BARCELONA TRAVEL GUIDE 2023

The Most Up-To-Date Pocket Guide to the City of Counts | Discover Barcelona's History, Art, Culture and Hidden Gems to Plan an Unforgettable Trip

By

Mike J. Darcey

© **Copyright 2023 - All rights reserved.**

The content contained within this book may not be reproduced, duplicated, or transmitted without direct written permission from the author or the publisher.

Under no circumstances will any blame or legal responsibility be held against the publisher, or author, for any damages, reparation, or monetary loss due to the information contained within this book. Either directly or indirectly.

Table of Contents

Introduction 3

Chapter 1: Things You Must Know About Barcelona ... 5

Chapter 2: Things You Can Only Do in Barcelona 25

Chapter 3: Best Places to Visit in Barcelona 36

Chapter 4: Itineraries 65

Chapter 5: Where To Stay in Barcelona 82

Chapter 6: Catalan Cuisine 84

Chapter 7: Where to Eat in Barcelona? 87

Chapter 8: Barcelona Nightlife, Entertainment and souvenirs. 92

Conclusion 103

Introduction

Barcelona, Spain. Here is a modern, multicultural city that has a lot to offer people with different tastes and personalities. The breathtaking architecture, the rich cuisine and fine wines, the lively atmosphere, and of course, the tranquil, laid-back way of life that makes everyone feel great!

Barcelona is a city rich in culture and history, and its intriguing past has helped to create the exciting, dynamic metropolis it is today. Barcelona has enough to offer visitors of all kinds, from early Roman towns to 20th-century modernist buildings.

Interesting Facts

Barcelona is a city full of intriguing details and undiscovered treasures. Here are a few interesting facts about this city you might not be aware of:

- FC Barcelona, the oldest football club in the world, was founded in Barcelona in 1899.

- La Rambla, the most well-known street in the city, is actually a collection of five distinct streets that have been connected over time.
- Over 135 years into its construction, Gaudi's beautiful Sagrada Familia is still not complete.
- Barcelona is renowned for its passion for all things culinary. More than 20 Michelin-starred restaurants, innumerable street food sellers, and classic tapas bars can all be found throughout the city.
- The city's beaches, such as Barceloneta and Nova Icaria, are well-liked by both residents and tourists and provide a pleasant break from the activity of the city center.
- There are many lovely parks in Barcelona, including the Parc de la Ciutadella, which houses the city's zoo, and the Parc Guell, which was created by Antoni Gaudi.
- The world-famous Magic Fountain of the city, which is situated in the Montjuic district, attracts tourists from all over the world with its amazing show of water, light, and music.

Barcelona has a long and fascinating past that has shaped the city in many ways. The city is a veritable gold mine of historical and cultural treasures, from its prehistoric Roman remains to its spectacular contemporary architecture.

Barcelona visitors have several options for learning about the city's past, from strolling through the Gothic Quarter's narrow lanes to admiring the Palau de la Musica Catalana's vibrant stained-glass windows.

Chapter 1: Things You Must Know About Barcelona

Barcelona's *Unique Culture and Identity*

The cultural and historical diversity of Barcelona, the capital of Catalonia, is outstanding. The mix of Spanish and Catalan influences that pervade the city's architecture, language, and customs is what gives it its distinct identity. This thriving metropolis attracts tourists from all over the world thanks to its rich cultural and architectural past, vibrant traditions, and modern, global culture.

Language and Identity

The official language of Catalonia, an autonomous region in northeastern Spain, is Catalan. While Spanish is the primary language in the city, Catalan is also frequently heard among the locals, and both languages are used on street signs and in public announcements. It is recommended for tourists to learn a few basic Catalan words in order to communicate with locals because this distinctive language feature contributes to Barcelona's distinctive cultural experience.

Architecture

Barcelona is renowned for its beautiful architecture, especially Antoni Gaud's creations. His unique Modernisme design is seen in well-known structures like La Sagrada Familia, Park Güell, Casa Batlló, and Casa Milà, which include organic shapes, vivid colors, and meticulous detailing. The Gothic Quarter, which has a maze of winding medieval alleyways and exquisitely maintained Gothic structures, adds to the city's architectural panorama.

Art and Museums

Art lovers will find a sanctuary in Barcelona. The city, which is home to the Picasso Museum and has a sizable collection of the artist's early works.

Traditions and Festivals

Barcelona is renowned for its exuberant festivals and distinctive customs. The city's yearly celebration honoring its patron saint, La Mercè, which takes place in September, is among the most well-known. The festival includes "castells," or human towers, live music, traditional Catalan dances like the "Sardana," and breathtaking fireworks displays. The Festa Major de Gràcia, Sant Jordi Day, and the exuberant Carnival celebrations are further noteworthy occasions.

Gastronomy

Barcelona's gastronomic scene is as vibrant and diversified as its cultural scene. Fresh Mediterranean ingredients are combined with distinctive flavors and cooking techniques in traditional Catalan cuisine. The city is also proud of its burgeoning tapas scene, where friends enjoy sharing small plates in buzzing pubs and eateries.

In conclusion, Barcelona's distinctive culture and personality are an alluring fusion of Catalan and Spanish influences, fine architecture, artistic treasures, active customs, and a flourishing cuisine scene. For those who want to fully immerse themselves in its diverse cultural landscape, this energetic city offers an absolutely memorable experience.

Understanding Catalans

Barcelona serves as the administrative center for the northeastern Spanish region of Catalonia. When traveling to the area, it's crucial to recognize and respect the distinctive culture and identity of the Catalan people.

Catalonia vs. Madrid

Political and cultural autonomy have long existed in Catalonia, and many Catalans take great pleasure in their history and sense of self. As a result, there are now disagreements between Catalonia and Madrid, the capital of Spain, with some Catalans calling for more autonomy or even independence.

Being mindful of these political and cultural issues is essential while communicating with Barcelona natives. The Spanish government and various facets of Spanish culture may be criticized by many Catalans who are proud of their ancestry. Politics and other delicate subjects are best avoided unless you are well-informed and capable of approaching the subject in a respectful and non-judgmental manner.

Dos and Don'ts

When interacting with locals in Barcelona, there are a few dos and don'ts to keep in mind to ensure that you show proper respect and appreciation for the local culture.

Dos:

- Do learn a few fundamental words and phrases in Spanish or Catalan, such "Hola" (hello) or "Gracias" (thank you). This demonstrates that you are making an effort to speak the locals' language.
- Do show courtesy and consideration, especially when meeting new people and visiting places of worship.
- Do sample some of the regional Spanish or Catalan dishes, such coca de recapte, paella, or tapas. Barcelona has a thriving food scene, and sampling regional cuisine is a terrific way to get a sense of the local way of life.
- When visiting cultural or religious sites like the Sagrada Familia or the Cathedral of Barcelona, dress appropriately. Typically, this entails covering your shoulders and legs and avoiding provocative or revealing attire.

Don'ts:

- Never assume that Spanish or Catalan is the native tongue of Barcelonans. There are additional languages spoken in the area, such as Aranese or Occitan, though most locals do speak one or both of them.
- Avoid being noisy or excessively loud in public. Barcelona is a lively and vibrant city, but it's also important to respect other people and keep the noise and behavior in public to a reasonable level.
- When trying to make plans or get directions, try not to be too pushy or insistent. Locals are typically affable and helpful, but excessively aggressive or demanding behavior may turn them off.

- Never presume that Barcelona residents have the same ideas or values as you. Like any major city, Barcelona is home to a variety of ethnic groups and cultures, so it's critical to approach every interaction with respect and an open mind.

You may fully appreciate the local culture and show appropriate respect for it by abiding by these dos and don'ts when visiting Barcelona.

Insider Tips for Tourists •

Etiquette

- **Greeting Etiquette:** Shaking hands with a stranger, friend, or business partner is practically required. You may have noticed that when greeting one another, locals frequently embrace, kiss, and shake hands.
- **Dining Etiquette:** Many Spanish restaurants offer designated smoking sections, while others have strict no smoking policies.

If you should be invited to dinner at someone's home, it's appropriate to bring a small present for the hostess (a bottle of wine, flowers, etc.) and, if they have them, a little something for the children.

- **Smoking Etiquette:** While many Spaniards smoke, smoking is now against the law in all public areas due to evolving legal regulations.

Time Zone

The time zone for Barcelona is UTC (universal time coordinated) + 1 hour. The time difference between Barcelona, Spain, and New York City is six hours (Barcelona is ahead on the clock). In Barcelona, it is 2:00 pm when it is 8:00 am in New York City.

The format for abbreviating dates in contrast to the US, Europe is different. Day, month, and year are used. Thus, August 23, 2019, is written as 23 August 2019, or 23/8/19, in Europe.

Saving Time & Money

- Using public transportation in Spain can lower the cost of getting around Barcelona. The Barcelona Card is something we wholeheartedly endorse! It allows you free access to public transit, free entrance to several tourist attractions, a range of discounts, and even the ability to bypass lines, all of which make getting around the city quite affordable and time efficient. It offers unquestionably great value: http://www.barcelonacard.org
- Consider renting an apartment if you want beachfront real estate without paying high hotel prices. You'll spend a lot less money and enjoy home comforts than if you stayed at a beachside hotel:

    http://www.tripadvisor.com/VacationRentals-g187497-Reviews-Barcelona_Catalonia-Vacation_Rentals.html

- To avoid paying more, we also always advise booking your flight, hotel room, show tickets, transportation, etc. as long in advance as you can. And if you can, avoid traveling between June and August, when tourism is at its highest.
- Save money by packing a picnic lunch by strolling down to Barcelona's Boqueria Food Market. Anybody can direct you there.
- Go to the museum on a free admission day! Like the first Sunday of every month is free at the Picasso Museum, and the first Wednesday of

every month is free at the Museum of Contemporary Culture.
- Take up ping pong! If money is tight, both families and groups of friends can have a good time in Barcelona at one of the many free ping-pong tables dotted across the city.

Tipping

In Barcelona, tipping is common but typically expected more from visitors than from residents. Most prices normally include service fees, although you might want to keep in mind that salaries are typically low.

- Taxi Drivers: Tipping is not customary, but if your driver went above and above to be kind and didn't transport you too far from your destination, you may wish to do so.
- Hotels: A tip of roughly €1 per suitcase is greatly appreciated for assistance with your luggage. If you stay for more than a few days and the chambermaid takes good care of your room, you can tip her a few euros. Room service is not expected to be tipped.
- Restaurants: In general, you can pay a few extra euros for a meal, but in more upmarket establishments, you should give 10-15% of the whole cost for good service.
- Tour guides: You can tip them between €5 and €10 per person if you liked the tour and thought the guide did a great job.

Information to know during your trip

Where are the services when you need to use the restroom in Barcelona? (Where can I find the restrooms?

The restrooms are referred to as *servicios*, *aseos*, or *lavabos*; for ladies, they are called *demas* or *seoras,* and for men, *caballeros*.

You should buy a Coke, coffee, or other modest item if you ask to use the restroom at a business that is exclusively open to paying customers.

Be mindful that not all restrooms you use will have soap or towels; in these cases, hand sanitizers will be useful.

Taxes

Pharmaceuticals, passenger transportation, entry to cultural and entertainment events, hotels, restaurants, and on consumables, medical supplies, and books all have reduced VAT rates.

If certain requirements are completed, foreign visitors may be entitled to a VAT refund: Firstly, you do not reside in Spain 2) You have to keep your receipts and have customs stamp your tax-free checks. 3) You have to show these to the bank issuing the VAT refund. 4) Purchases must be more than the usual minimum of €90.15.

Making calls

Spain's country code is 34.

Dial 00 first while calling home from Barcelona. The tone will then start.

Electricity

In Spain, as in the rest of Europe, the average voltage is 220-230 volts, with an average frequency of 50 cycles per second (to compare, the U.S. averages 110 volts, alternating at about 60 cycles per second.) As was previously mentioned, you will need to pack an adaptor and converter if you are coming from outside of Europe in order to use your devices and appliances in the appropriate outlets.

You only need an adaptor to be able to plug in cell phone, tablet, and laptop chargers because they are frequently dual voltage devices. Most small appliances are probably dual voltage.

In an emergency

There are more emergency numbers in Spain in addition to the 112 (which can be called in English, Italian, French, or German). In Barcelona, you can also call the police at 091, an ambulance at 061, and the fire department at 080 in case of an emergency.

Spanish Phrases for Emergencies:

No entiendo	I don't understand
Por favor mandeme una Ambulancia.	Please send me an ambulance.
Por favor envie ayuda inmediatamente.	Please send help immediately.
Socorro!	Help!
Por favor, llame a la policía.	Please call the police.
Me siento mal.	I don't feel well.
Cuánto cuesta?	How much does it cost?

Common Spanish Phrases

Hola – "Hello"
- *Me llamo…* – "My name is…"
- *¿Y tú?* – "And you?"
- *Mucho gusto* – "Nice to meet you"

- *¿Qué tal?* – "How are you?"
- *Nos vemos* – "See you"
- *Por favor* – "Please"
- *Gracias* – "Thank you"
- *De nada* – "You're welcome"
- *Disculpa* (informal "you") / *disculpe* (formal "you") – "Excuse me"
- *Me gusta / No me gusta…* – "I like / I don't like…"
- *¿Cuánto cuesta?* – "How much is this?"
- *¿Dónde está el baño?* – "Where's the bathroom?"
- *¿Qué hora es?* – "What time is it?"
- *Me puede ayudar, por favor* – "Can you help me, please?" (formal "you")

simply ask a staff member at your hotel or other place of lodging to point you in the direction of the closest pharmacy (farmàcia) for any minor medical difficulties (cold, flu, etc.). They are identified by a green cross.

Holidays

Main Public Holidays in Barcelona (banks, government services and most shops and museums close, but most restaurants, cafés and bars stay open):

- January 1 — New Year's Day (Any Nou)
- January 6 — Three Kings Day (Reis Magos)
- April (dates vary) — Good Friday (Divendres Sant), Easter, Easter Monday (Dilluns de Pasqua)
- May 1 — May Day - Labour Day (Festa del Treball)
- June 1 — Fiesta Local (Segona Pascua)
- June 24 — Sant Joan - St. John
- August 15 — Verge de l'Assumpció
- September 11 — National Day Catalunya (Diada de Catalunya)
- September 24 — La Mercè
- October 12 — Spain National Day

- November 1 — All Saints' Day (Tots Sants)
- December 6 — Constitution Day (Día de la Constitución)
- December 8 — La Immaculada
- December 25 — Christmas Day (Nadal)
- December 26 — Boxing Day (Sant Esteve)

Please be aware that cab fares are typically higher on holidays in Barcelona and that, if the holiday comes on a Thursday or Tuesday, many Spaniards will "build a bridge" and take Friday or Monday off as well, extending the weekend.

Hours of Operation

In Barcelona, restaurants are typically closed on Sunday evenings and Mondays. In August, some restaurants close for two to three weeks as locals take vacations.

Barcelona's banks are open from 8:30 am to 1:00 or 2:00 pm, Monday through Friday. ATMs are always accessible across the city.

In Barcelona, many museums and other tourist attractions are closed on Mondays, but not all of them. Many other tourist destinations, including La Pedrera and Parc Güell, are still open.

Depending on the store, shops normally open from 9:00 am to 1:30 pm, close for lunch, then reopen from 4:30 to 8:00, 9:00, or 11:00 night.

On Monday through Friday, post offices are normally open from 9:00 am to 2:00 pm.

Money

The euro (€/ EUR) is Spain's official currency, as we have mentioned.

It's preferable to keep your cash always carrying capacity between €150 and €200. This will lessen your losses in the event of loss or theft.

Additionally, it's best to use the city's non-touristy ATMs and tellers. Also, use common sense to avoid becoming a pickpocket target. If someone unexpectedly comes up to you, it's best to politely move on.

Also, beware of pointless charges. Say no if you're given the choice to pay with your credit card in dollars rather than euros. You will pay higher fees when paying in dollars, and you could or might not be made aware of them at the time of the transaction.

How to Avoid Lines and Select the Top Tours in Barcelona

Barcelona experiences heavy visitor traffic, and you can face exceptionally long lineups at popular attractions like the Sagrada Familia and Park Guell. Buy your tickets online at GetyourGuide. to avoid the lines and save an average of 20 minutes per line.

Ideal Season to Visit

Barcelona is a well-liked tourist destination all year round thanks to its pleasant Mediterranean climate, plethora of historical sites, beautiful architecture, and cultural attractions. Depending on your tastes, you can visit Barcelona during any of the following seasons:

Peak Season (June - August)

June, July, and August during the summer are regarded as Barcelona's peak season. With usual highs of 25-30°C (77-86°F), the weather is nice and sunny at this time of year. The beaches are a popular destination for vacationers, and the city is hopping with festivals, concerts, and cultural events. The busiest and most expensive time of year to travel is summer due to the large number of people and higher hotel and activity prices. You must make reservations in advance if you wish to visit during peak hours.

High Season (November - February)

The cooler and less crowded months of November through February are considered Barcelona's low season. If you want to avoid the crowds and get better discounts on flights and lodging, this is a wonderful time to travel. However, due to the weather, some attractions and eateries might be closed at this time, and outdoor activities might be restricted (March - May and September - October)

Barcelona's shoulder seasons are from March through May and from September through October. The weather is mild and pleasant throughout this period, with typical temperatures between 16 and 22 °C (61 and 72 °F). In comparison to the busy season, there are less people and reduced lodging and activity costs. If you want to take advantage of outdoor activities like hiking or cycling, or if you want to enjoy the city's cultural and historical attractions without the crowds, now is a great time to visit. The drawback of traveling in the shoulder season is that the weather can be erratic; therefore, it is important to bring clothes and be ready for the possibility of sporadic rain.

Overall, your interests and priorities will determine the best time to visit Barcelona. The high season might be your best bet if you don't mind the crowds and want to take advantage of the city's festivities and beaches. The low season might be more to your taste if you want a quieter, more reasonably priced vacation. The shoulder season is the best time to travel if you want to get the best of all worlds—good weather, fewer tourists, and cheaper prices. Barcelona is a city that has something to offer everyone at any time of year thanks to its diverse cultural history, exciting nightlife, and beautiful architecture.

How to dress: what to pack

Winter: You won't need a lot of anti-cold gear throughout the winter in Barcelona; a sweater and jeans will be sufficient. However, keep in mind that when you are near the water, it is always humid, so wearing thermal underwear and a thick jacket is never a bad idea.

In the summer, you should pack everything you need for the beach, and sandals, t-shirts, and shorts will do for evening dress. Even in the hottest locations, having a jacket or lightweight jacket on hand might be essential because rain is a constant possibility.

In the fall and spring: You may experience frequent rainy days in the fall, so always take an umbrella and wear in layers with jackets, sweatshirts, and shirts that are waterproof. The dress recommendations for spring, on the other hand, are a mix of autumn and summer because spring is moderate but may still come with some surprises. Lightweight clothing, such as t-shirts and long sleeve shirts, worn with a sweatshirt or jacket. In terms of footwear, bring a few raincoats along but generally opt for sandals, ankle boots, or sneakers.

Barcelona's transportation system

Options for Public Transportation

Visitors can easily explore the city and its surroundings thanks to Barcelona's extensive and effective public transportation system. The metro, buses, trams, and local trains are the main modes of public transportation.

Metro The Metro in Barcelona is the easiest and fastest way to get around the city. There are 8 lines total, labeled L1 through L5 and L9 through L11, respectively. The metro operates from 5:00 am to midnight on weekdays; on weekends and holidays, the hours are extended.

The large bus network of **Buses** Barcelona serves the entire city and is comprised of more than 100 routes run by TMB. A limited overnight bus service dubbed NitBus runs from 10:00 pm to 5:00 am, but buses normally run from 5:00 am to 11:00 pm.

Trams Their system consists of two networks (Trambaix and Trambess), provides service to sections of the city that the metro does not cover, primarily in the west and east. On weekdays, trams typically operate from 5:00 am until midnight, with longer hours on weekends and holidays.

For tram routes, schedules, and maps, visit the **Tram Barcelona** website: https://www.tram.cat

Local Trains (Rodalies) The **Rodalies de Catalunya** Local trains link Barcelona with surrounding cities including Sitges, Girona, and Montserrat as well as its suburbs. Trains are a great way to get around the area and run often.

For information on train routes, schedules, and fares, visit the **Rodalies de Catalunya** website:

https://www.rodalies.gencat.cat

Tickets and Prices A single metro, bus, or tram ticket costs €2.40. To save money, guests can buy a T-Casual card, which costs €11.35 for 10 trips. Within Zone 1, the T-Casual card is accepted on the metro, buses, trams, and Rodalies trains.

Consider the Hola Barcelona Travel Card for extended stays or unlimited travel. For 2, 3, 4, or 5 days, it offers unrestricted use of public transit. A 2-day card costs as little as €16.30 and may be purchased online or at metro stations.

In conclusion, Barcelona's public transportation choices, which include the metro, buses, trams, and local trains, offer a practical and reasonably priced means to explore the city and its surrounds. By making use of these services, tourists can reduce their environmental effect while having a local's perspective on the city.

Taxis and Rideshares

In Barcelona, ridesharing services and taxis are commonly available for people who prefer a more direct and adaptable means of transportation. These solutions can be particularly helpful after midnight when public transit may be scarce or nonexistent.

Taxis

Taxis in Barcelona can be recognized by their distinctive black and yellow color scheme. They can be reserved in advance, located at designated taxi ranks, or flagged down on the street. All taxis have meters, and there may be extra fees for services like luggage pickup from the airport or late-night service. In general, taxis in Barcelona are regarded as trustworthy and secure.

Several taxi companies operate in the city, including:

- **Radio Taxi 033**: +34 933 033 033
- **Fono Taxi**: +34 933 300 300
- **Barna Taxi**: +34 933 577 755

Rideshares Uber and Cabify, two well-known ride-sharing services, offer service in Barcelona. Through these apps, users can order a ride and pay for it immediately. Since they offer an estimated fare and arrival time as well as the option to track the driver's location, rideshare services may be more practical than taxis.

Download the corresponding apps from the Google Play (Android) or App Store (iOS) to use these services:

- Uber: https://www.uber.com
- Cabify: https://www.cabify.com

Local Taxi and Rideshare Apps Numerous regional apps allow users to reserve taxis or shared rides in Barcelona in addition to international ridesharing services. These applications frequently offer a comparable service to Uber and Cabify while also helping nearby companies:

- **Free Now:** Free Now is a well-liked taxi booking app in Barcelona that provides fixed rates, driver tracking, and the capability to make payments directly from the app. Download for free right now from the Google Play store or the App Store for iOS: https://free-now.com
- **Yego**: Yego is an app with a basis in Barcelona that provides shared electric mopeds as a green substitute for conventional taxis or rideshares. Through the app, users can find, reserve, and unlock nearby mopeds. Yego can be downloaded from Google Play or the App Store for iOS devices:

  https://www.rideyego.com

Biking and Walking the City

Barcelona is a small, walkable city, making it convenient and pleasurable to explore its sights on foot. Many of its neighborhoods, including the Gothic Quarter, El Raval, and El Born, are best explored on foot because slowing down allows you to fully appreciate their historic charm and narrow streets.

In addition to walking, biking is a well-liked and environmentally friendly method of getting around the city. Visitors may easily rent bikes and pedal safely about the city thanks to Barcelona's well-developed network of bike lanes and its bike-sharing program.

Shared Bike System (Bicing), Barcelona's public bike-sharing program, is primarily intended for city residents, while it is also accessible to tourists staying in the city for an extended amount of time. The program, which enables users to borrow bikes from specified stations throughout the city, requires registration online and a monthly cost. On the Bicing website, you may register and find out more information.: https://www.bicing.barcelona

Bike Rentals The cost of renting a city bike varies based on the model of bike and the length of the rental, but is often between €6 and €10 for two hours or €12 to €20 for a full day. Several well-known bike rental businesses in Barcelona include:

- **Barcelona Rent a Bike**: https://www.barcelonarentabike.com
- **Green Bikes Barcelona**: https://www.greenbikesbarcelona.com
- **Budget Bikes**: https://www.budgetbikes.eu

Bike Tours Bike tours with a guide are yet another fantastic way to see the city. These excursions frequently include stops at well-known locations and insider knowledge from a knowledgeable guide about the area. Reputable bicycle tour providers in Barcelona include:

- **Fat Tire Tours**: https://www.fattiretours.com/barcelona
- **Steel Donkey Bike Tours**: https://www.steeldonkeybiketours.com
- **Barcelona eBikes**: https://www.barcelonaebikes.com

Car Rentals and Driving Tips

While taking the bus, walking, or riding a bike are frequently the most practical ways to see Barcelona, some tourists might prefer the flexibility of renting a car, particularly when organizing day trips or excursions to nearby locations. However, it's crucial to take into account the difficulties of driving in a crowded, foreign city, as well as parking regulations and expenses.

Renting a car At Barcelona-El Prat Airport and in the city's center, there are offices for a number of international and local car rental companies. Popular choices comprise:

- **Hertz**: https://www.hertz.com
- **Avis**: https://www.avis.com
- **Europcar**: https://www.europcar.com
- **Sixt**: https://www.sixt.com

A valid driver's license, a credit card for the security deposit, and occasionally an international driving permit are required in order to rent a car (IDP). To assure availability and the best prices, it is advised to make your vehicle rental reservations in advance.

Driving Tips

Barcelona's congested roads, narrow streets, and complicated road system can make driving difficult. Observe the following advice to ensure a safe and enjoyable driving experience:

1. Keep an eye out for differences in road markings, speed limits, and traffic signs from your home country.
2. Using a GPS You can more simply and safely traverse Barcelona's streets with the aid of a dependable GPS or guidance program.
3. Avoid peak hours: Morning and evening rush hours can be extremely congested in Barcelona (approximately 7:00-9:00 am and 5:00-8:00 pm). In order to avoid tension and delays, plan your trip hours accordingly.

4. Be wary of restricted areas: Barcelona has a number of APRs, or Areas of Priority Residential, where only residents, approved cars, and public transportation are permitted to drive. To avoid penalties, exercise caution in these areas.
5. Develop patience: Try to maintain composure and patience while driving in a crowded metropolis, especially when confronted with unforeseen circumstances or aggressive drivers.

Parking

1. 1.Due to the scarcity of street parking and the high cost of parking garages, parking in Barcelona can be difficult. Here are some pointers for parking in the city:
2. 2.Green and blue zones: With a stay limit of 1-4 hours, on-street parking is accessible in specified blue and green zones. At nearby parking meters, daytime hours (typically 9:00 am to 8:00 pm) require payment.
3. 3.Parking lots: There are private parking garages across the city, but the costs can be high— between €3 and €5 per hour or €20 and €40 per day. For guests, certain hotels may offer subsidized or free parking.
4. 4.Park-and-ride: If you won't be using your car while visiting Barcelona, think about leaving it at a park-and-ride location outside the city and use public transportation to get around.

Chapter 2: Things You Can Only Do in Barcelona

Have dinner and stroll on Las Ramblas

Las Ramblas is Barcelona's main tourist destination. Along this 1.2-kilometer pedestrian strip, there are many gift shops, cafes, restaurants, hawkers, and street performers.

The most famous promenade in the city, Las Ramblas, is typically busy with curious tourists no matter what time of day you arrive. While touring Las Ramblas during the day is intriguing, doing it at night is considerably more fun, especially when the street performers and artists begin their stunning displays early in the evening.

Exploring Las Ramblas is without a doubt the best way to begin a night in Barcelona. You can unwind with a drink at one of the several local bars or restaurants after strolling down the renowned boulevard and giving a round of applause to the top street entertainers.

Here are a few of Las Ramblas' most popular attractions:

Erotica Museum

Address:La Rambla, 96 bis

Phone:+34 933 18 98 65

Barcelona Wax Museum

Address:Passatge de la Banca, 7

Phone:+34 933 17 26 49

Modernist Boqueria Market

Address:La Rambla, 91

Phone:+34 933 18 25 84

Christopher Columbus Monument

Address:Plaça Portal de la pau, s/n

Phone:+34 932 85 38 32

White Painter Statue

Address:Passeig de Colom, s/n

The Joan Miro mosaic is also located within Las Ramblas' promenade. There are several flower stores where you may discover distinctive and fresh flowers.

Additionally, allotting some time to tour La Boquera is essential. One of the oldest markets in Spain and Barcelona is this one. A vast range of fruits are available. Buying the customary chorizo and sausages is also essential. Don't forget to take in the market's stunning stained glass and Art Nouveau buildings as well.

Ride the "Steel Donkey".

Of course, a bicycle is referred to as a "steel donkey" in this context. In Barcelona, you can go on a bicycle tour.

The Steel Donkey Bike Tour, however, is not your typical cycling excursion.

A Steel Donkey Bike Tour will take you through the quaint backstreets of El Bourne, the historic industrial ruins of Poblenou, and the Gracia village district. While on this bike trip, you can see a ton of flea markets, squat dwellings, and recycled workshops.

Address:The Green Bike Shop, Carrer Ample 53

Phone:+34 657286854

Email: info@steeldonkeybiketours.com

Get Electric on A Bicycle

You can take an e-bike trip in addition to the traditional Steel Donkey Bike tour. It is an exciting experience that allows you to race alongside city traffic.

Address:Carrer de Montsió, 10

Phone:+34 902 02 77 20

See Madonna on a Magic Hill

In Barcelona, you can see the statue of the Virgin Mary known as the Black Madonna. In the lofty peaks of Montserrat Mountain, this statue can be found at the Montserrat Abbey. To see this statue, a large number of pilgrims travel to the high mountains from all over the world. But there are a lot of other reasons why people visit Montserrat Mountain. The view from this "jagged" mountain is stunning. A wine tour is another option close to the Montserrat peak.

Phone:+34 938 77 77 77

Go on a Barcelona Booze Cruise

On a Barcelona Booze Cruise, you may indulge in sailor-style drinking! On a Barcelona Booze Cruise, you may savor delectable grilled food, beer, sangria, and mixed drinks. Games and the music of the resident DJs are also available. Party animals should take the Barcelona Booze Cruise.

Phone:(+34)602 660 736

Drive a Ferrari Around an F1 Circuit

It is not every day that you get to drive a Ferrari and it is definitely not every day that you get to drive around the Circuit de Catalunya which is the official track of the Spanish F1 Grand Prix. Well, the good news is, you can do this in Barcelona. You can also pretend that you are James Bond while you are driving on the way to Monte Carl.

Address:Camino Mas Moreneta

Phone:938864451

You don't get to drive a Ferrari every day, and you certainly don't get to race around the Circuit de Catalunya, the official track of the Spanish F1 Grand Prix. The good thing is that Barcelona allows you to do this. While you are driving to Monte Carlo, you can also imagine that you are James Bond.

Dine in a Dark Area

Not just any restaurant, though, is Dance Le Noir. You will eat dinner in a dark room at this restaurant, which will provide for a wonderful sensory experience. The majority of the staff at the restaurant is blind. If you want to try something new with your friends, you should enjoy dinner at Dance Le Noir? because the food is excellent. This restaurant offers a great experience for dining.

Address:Passeig de Picasso, 10

Phone:+34 932 68 70 17

Cover your body with chocolate!

Barcelona is a jovial city. In Barcelona, getting a massage is a necessity. In this city, you can get a variety of massages. The well-known chocolate massage is an option. You'll be able to feel what it's like to be coated in chocolate thanks to this! The massage using seashells is another option.

Address:Carrer de Mallorca, 180

Phone:+34 930 00 91 65

Go on a Treasure Hunt

In Barcelona, you may go on a treasure hunt. You may stroll around Barri Gotic's twisting streets thanks to this enjoyable activity. A bottle of Spanish wine is yours as a prize if you prevail.

Address:Plaça dels Pirineus, 3-4

Phone:+34 932 80 92 74

info@bcn-adventure.com

Explore the Beautiful Park Guell

The Park Guell is a wonderful location for a picnic. Inside the park, there are many tourist attractions. Within the park is a municipal garden. Additionally, you may see "El Drac," a stunning mosaic salamander designed by Gaudi.

The following are some of the sights you ought to see when at Park Guell:

- The Viaduct
- The Pavilion
- The Colonaded Pathway
- The Ceiling Mosaic in Hypostyle Room
- The Bird Nests

Phone:+34 902 20 03 02

Enjoy the Magic Fountain Show

This is a "must see" sight in Barcelona. The Font Magica Fountain is unlike any other fountain you've ever seen. In 1929, this fountain was constructed. This fountain receives about 2 million visitors each year.

Address:Plaça de Carles Buïgas, 1

Enjoy the Camp Nou Experience and FC Barcelona Museum

Nothing compares to seeing Barcelona play at home. You should, however, also go to the FC Barcelona Museum. The largest Nike stores in the entire world are located at Camp Nou. On game days, stalls outside the stadium sell reasonably priced FCB scarves and T-shirts.

Address:C. Aristides Maillol, 12

Phone:+34 902 18 99 00

Discover unique and fantastic modernist buildings.

In Barcelona, you will come across a lot of stunning and breathtaking modernist structures. If you visit Barcelona, you should visit these structures:

Casa Amatler

Address:Passeig de Gràcia, 41

Phone:+34 932 16 01 75

Casa Mila

Address:Provença, 261-265

Phone:+34 902 20 21 38

Casa Batillo

Address:Passeig de Gràcia, 43

Phone:+34 932 16 03 06

The Casa Batillo is one of Spain's most exquisite structures. The renowned Antoni Gaudi created it. In actuality, it is one of his greatest works. It is situated in Barcelona's center.

Another fascinating modernist structure is Casa Mila. It also goes by the name La Pedrera. Josep Maria Jujol and Antoni Gaudi collaborated in its design.

Casa Amatler is a unique, modernist building designed by Josep Puig Cadafalch. The design is a mix of Catalan and Flemish style.

Tour inside the Sagrada Familia

The Sagrada Familia is unparalleled. It is among the most distinctive and well-known buildings in the entire world. The world-famous architect Antoni Gaudi was responsible for the design of this spectacular church, which was built in 1882.

Taste Your Way Around the City

The love of Spanish people for eating and spending time at the table is well known. It is not advised to visit Barcelona without having a memorable experience with both local and national cuisine.

There are several excellent local bars in the city where you may indulge in a delicious glass of cava while eating the city's famous tapas. Bar Pinotxo, which is located in the renowned La Boqueria's food market, is one of the top tapas bars. Whether you want to indulge in some soft baby squid, try some local potatoes, or taste the caramel-sweet pork belly, this location will satisfy you because it serves all of these and many other tapas in a friendly setting. Simply give it a shot!

Indulge in the Delicious Cava

The Spanish are renowned for appreciating their food, but they are also well-known for enjoying booze. Catalans also enjoy gin and sangria, as well as cava and fragrant vermouth.

When visiting Barcelona, you must sample the Catalan cava, which is similar to fine champagne. This is the ideal beverage to enjoy after a leisurely brunch, late breakfast, or filling lunch at a nearby restaurant.

Visit La Vinya del Senyor, a welcoming neighborhood restaurant, for some of the greatest cava in the area. They serve delectable cava by the glass. Don't overindulge in alcohol over lunch because you still have enough to see and do!

Another typical beverage in Catalonia is vermouth. It can be served with an orange slice as a garnish and some delectable green olives. On a beautiful weekend, picture yourself wandering around the streets of Barcelona. In the afternoon, you'll notice that every bar is crowded with people having a good time with their friends while sipping on this delectable aperitif. Consider joining them.

Visit Morro Fi if you want to visit a pub noted for its delectable vermouth. Simply take a seat, request a recommendation from the bartender, and wait for the best "vermut" to be delivered to your table.

La Vinya del Senyor is located in Plaza Sta Maria, 5, in Barcelona, Spain. It is open from 12 p.m. to 1 a.m., 12 a.m. to 2 a.m., and 12 a.m. to 12 a.m. on weekends. Its phone number is 933 10 33 79.

Morro Fi's address is Carrer del Consell de Cent, 171 in Barcelona, Spain, and its hours are 12 to 4 on weekdays and 12 to 4 on weekends.

Relax on the Beach

In Barcelona, you will witness some of the liveliest beaches, even though you won't find the beaches of your dreams, with wonderful natural beauty and hiking routes. There isn't a more relaxing activity than a picnic on the sand. Since this is where all the action is, you can grab some delectable food from the La Boqueria food market and head straight to La Barceloneta. Simply relax, eat what you want, drink some local wine, and take in the diverse array of beachgoers as you listen to the waves crash.

La Barceloneta is an excellent location for tourists who are staying in the city for a few days. If you intend to stay longer, you should find a more remote location, such as Montgat or Castelldefels, where you can enjoy the beach as the locals do, away from all the vendors. If you have the time, you should visit these stunning beaches that are located outside of the city.

From late May to early October, when the sea is warm enough to be enjoyable, is the greatest time to go swimming in Barcelona. The water is usually between 21 and 27 degrees Celsius at this period, making swimming, diving, and other water sports enjoyable.

Top Beaches:

Beautiful beaches can be found throughout Barcelona and are well-liked by both locals and tourists. The following are a few of Barcelona's top beaches:

One of the most well-known beaches in the city is Barceloneta Beach, which is close to the city's core. The beach has soft sand, crystal-clear water, and a selection of eateries and cafes.

Bogatell Beach is a less-frequented option that is quieter and situated in the Poblenou district. The beach is renowned for its tranquil seas and welcoming atmosphere for families.

Another well-liked option is Nova Icaria Beach, which is close to the Olympic Village. Long stretches of sandy beach, crystal-clear water, and a variety of facilities, such as showers and restrooms, can be found at the beach.

Have Lunch in the Park

On a nice day in Barcelona, you must have a lovely picnic in Ciutadella Park. People are constantly gathered in the park reading, talking with friends, or simply gazing up at the sky to unwind.

The park is pleasant, allowing you to sit on the grass and enjoy your dinner, whether you just want to indulge in some delectable fruits you got at the farmer's market or you want to have a glass of cava and some delectable Spanish cheese.

Explore the City on a Moto

Barcelona is exceptionally well connected, so you can easily catch the train or meander about its streets on foot if you feel the need to leave the busy city center. However, if you want to see the city like a local and go through its most interesting streets, you must rent a moto.

For the less powerful ones, you can drive without a license, and there are a surprising number of locations where you can rent a scooter that is simple to operate. You will enjoy joining the throngs of people on two wheels that fill the streets of Barcelona. Just take care to avoid the highway as it can be dangerous. Otherwise, you can see the entire city more quickly and have a great time doing it, especially if you do it with a friend!

Exploring Dali's beloved Figueres and strolling through Old Girona

Barcelona is one of the top vacation spots for lovers of art and architecture, not just because wandering the city is like entering the brilliant mind of Gaudi, but also because Picasso was quite familiar with the region and because it is where some of Miro's best works are located.

Furthermore, the vibrant city is not distant from Figueres, a Catalan town best renowned for holding the Teatre-Museu Dal. If you want to understand surrealism better and appreciate Dali's ability, you must visit the museum. Visitors can also enjoy the fascinating Modernista architecture and the lovely Castell de Sant Ferran, both of which date back to the 18th century, in Figueres.

If you're not into art, you could be interested in visiting one of Girona's medieval borders, which is home to one of Europe's oldest Jewish communities. History buffs from all over the world are drawn to Girona by its legacy and fall in love with its beautiful gardens, winding lanes, and little streets.

Given that there are just 128 kilometers between Barcelona and Girona, the drive takes only about 1:30 hours. From Girona to Figueres, there are only 44 more kilometers, but the journey is worthwhile. On their way back to Barcelona, most visitors to Figueres make a pit stop in Girona and spend the second half of the day exploring its lovely streets.

Chapter 3: Best Places to Visit in Barcelona

1.Casa Mila

Entry is 27 euros ($21.6 with the Barcelona Card). The office is open from Monday through Friday from 9 am to 6 pm and from 10 am to 2 pm on the weekends.

The Eixample district of Barcelona is home to the well-known modernist building Casa Mila, also known as La Pedrera. One of the city's most iconic landmarks is Casa Mila, a modernist architectural marvel designed by renowned architect Antoni Gaudi and completed in 1912.

History: Pere Mila, a successful businessman, and his wife, Roser Segimon, commissioned the structure because they desired a distinctive and modern home for themselves and their renters. Gaudi was selected as the project's architect, and he worked on the structure for six years, until it was finished in 1912.

Visitors' details:

The public is welcome to visit Casa Mila, where they can examine the distinctive architecture and design of the structure and discover more about Gaudi's life and legacy. Daily hours of operation for the building change depending on the season. Adult admission is about €22, with reductions offered to children, students, and older citizens.

Interesting Features

The following are a some of the most intriguing sights and activities in Casa Mila:

The rooftop terrace of Casa Mila is embellished with distinctive chimney stacks and sculptural forms and gives breathtaking views of the city.

The Espai Gaudi is a museum devoted to Antoni Gaudi's creations. It houses a collection of his original drawings and plans as well as pictures and models of some of his most well-known structures.

The flat: Complete with authentic furniture and décor, visitors can explore a typical apartment from the early 20th century.

What to Notice: There are a number of things about Casa Mila that are distinctive. These include:

The stone facade has a wave-like or sand-dune-like pattern to it.

The seaweed-inspired, twisted balcony railings made of wrought iron.

Gaudi's signature style is evident in the building's organic curves and contours.

In conclusion, Casa Mila is a fascinating and essential tourist destination for everyone interested in Antoni Gaudi's work and modernist architecture. It will undoubtedly be the highlight of any vacation to Barcelona with to its distinctive design, intriguing displays, and breathtaking city vistas.

2. Casa Calvet

Another stunning piece of architecture in the center of Barcelona is Casa Calvet. The structure, which Antoni Gaudi designed and finished in 1900, is a wonderful representation of the designer's distinctive style and is recommended for anybody with an interest in modernist construction.

History:

Pere Màrtir Calvet, a maker of textiles, had Casa Calvet constructed as a private property. The structure was completed in 1900 after three years of work by Gaudi, who had been hired for the project in 1898. Calvet, the building's first owner, is honored by its name.

Visitor Information:

Visitors can still enjoy Casa Calvet's distinctive architecture and design from the outside even though the building's interior isn't accessible to the general public. The structure is situated in Barcelona's Eixample neighborhood and is visible from the street.

Interesting Things:

Although Casa Calvet is only visible from the outside, there are still several intriguing features to note about the structure, including:

- The building's facade, which contrasts with Gaudi's later works in more traditional design. It has features like stone cornices, wrought iron balconies, and ornate stonework around the windows and doorways.
- The rooftop's architecture, which features a dome and a rooftop patio, is reminiscent of other Gaudi-designed structures.
- The elaborate doorway features a statue of St. George defeating the dragon, which is a representation of Catalonia.

What to Notice:

There are various features of Casa Calvet that stand out when viewed from the street, including:

- the use of various materials to give the facade's texture, such as stone, wrought iron, and glazed tiles.
- the elaborate window and entryway decorations, which feature floral designs and exquisite woodwork.
- the sculptures that adorn the doorway, including the busts of Pere Màrtir Calvet and his son.

Although guests are not permitted inside Casa Calvet, the structure's distinctive architecture and design are nevertheless worth observing from the outside. It is an important example of Antoni Gaudi's early work, offers an intriguing look at the architect's developing style, and is a must-see for anybody interested in architecture who is traveling to Barcelona.

3.Guell Palace

$12 for admission Winter hours* are Tuesday through Sunday from 10 a.m. to 5.30 p.m.

History:

Eusebi Guell, a successful entrepreneur and Gaudi's supporter, ordered the palace. Guell commissioned Gaudi to create a lavish family home that would reflect his wealth and social standing. Gaudi worked on the project for more for 20 years, finally finishing it in 1890.

Visitors' details:

Guell Palace is now a public museum where anyone may explore the distinctive architecture of the structure and discover more about Gaudi's life and work. The museum has daily hours that change depending on the season. Adult admission is about €12, with reductions offered to children, students, and older citizens.

Interesting Features

The following are a few of the most intriguing sights and activities in Guell Palace:

- The magnificent entrance hall welcomes guests with elaborate embellishments, including a huge stained-glass skylight and elaborate ironwork.
- The roof terrace is embellished with ceramic tile-covered chimneys and ventilation towers that resemble vibrant medieval helmets.
- The welcome area: The reception area is a lavish chamber with finely carved oak ceilings and mosaic tiled walls.
- What to Notice: There are a number of things about Guell Palace that are distinctive. These include:
- the application of many elements, including glass, iron, and stone, which gives the facade a rich and varied texture.
- The building's elaborate elements, which include carved woodwork, mosaic tiles, and vibrant stained glass.

- the creative way in which space and light were used, such as the central courtyard and the inside skylights.

Overall, Guell Palace is a must-see for anyone interested in Antoni Gaudi's work and modernist architecture. It will undoubtedly be a highlight of any vacation to Barcelona with to its distinctive design, intriguing displays, and exquisite workmanship.

4.Casa Batllo

Entry is $22.5 ($19.5 with the Barcelona Card) and is open Monday through Sunday from 9 am to 9 pm.

Another magnificent illustration of Antoni Gaudi's distinctive architectural style is Casa Batllo. The building, which is in the center of Barcelona's Eixample neighborhood, is a well-liked destination for both tourists and fans of architecture.

History:

The structure was first built in 1877, but Gaudi later had it renovated between 1904 and 1906 for the affluent Batllo family. The building's facade was altered by Gaudi, who added a quirky and vibrant design that has made it one of Barcelona's most famous landmarks.

Visitors' details:

Today, Casa Batllo is accessible to the general public, where guests can explore the structure's distinctive architecture and design and discover more about Gaudi's life and legacy. Daily hours of operation for the building change depending on the season. Adult admission is about €28, with reductions offered to children, students, and older citizens.

Interesting Features

The following are a few of the most intriguing sights and activities in Casa Batllo:

- The building's undulating front is decorated with a colorful mosaic made from shattered ceramic tiles, giving the facade a wave-like appearance.
- The rooftop terrace of Casa Batllo is embellished with distinctive chimney stacks and sculptural forms and gives breathtaking views of the city.
- Visitors are welcome to tour the interior of the building, especially the Noble Floor, which has been restored to its original design and boasts distinctive elements like stained glass windows and vibrant tiles.
- What to Notice: There are a number of things about Casa Batllo that are distinctive. These include:
- the way in which space, light, and color are used to provide visitors a rich, immersive experience.
- the sculpture-like features seen throughout the structure, such as the dragon-like roof and the curved facade.
- the minute particulars, such the vibrant tiles, stained glass windows, and wrought iron balconies.

5. Sagrada Familia

Entry costs 15 euros (or 14 euros with the Barcelona Card) and is available from 9 am to 8 pm.

The Sagrada Familia is perhaps Barcelona's most well-known monument and one of the most distinctive and stunning churches in the entire world. It is a must-see destination for anybody traveling to Barcelona and was created by Antoni Gaudi. It is situated in the city's Eixample neighborhood.

History:

The Sagrada Familia is still being built today, with a projected completion date of 2026. Construction started in 1882. The project was taken over by Antoni Gaudi in 1883, and he worked on it nonstop for the remainder of his life using his original designs and plans.

Visitor Information:

There are numerous tour options available at the Sagrada Familia, including guided tours, audio tours, and tower tours. Because the monument frequently sells out and there can be lengthy lines, visitors are advised to buy tickets in advance. The entrance cost, which includes access to the nave and museum, ranges from €20 to €40 depending on the type of ticket.

Tips:
- In order to guarantee availability and avoid long waits, buy your tickets in advance.
- To find out more about the monument's significance and history, think considering joining a guided tour.
- By going early in the morning or late in the day, you can avoid the throng.
- When visiting the church, observe the dress code and decorum, which includes covering your shoulders and knees and not talking aloud or taking pictures during mass.

Interesting Things:

The following are a few of the most intriguing sights and activities in the Sagrada Familia:

- The church's spectacular front is decorated with elaborate carvings and sculptures that show scenes from Jesus' life and those of other religious luminaries.
- The church's interior is decorated with vibrant stained glass windows that give the space a special and majestic feel.
- Visitors can ascend to the top of the Nativity Tower to take in breathtaking views of the city and get a closer look at the distinctive architecture of the structure.

What to Notice:

- There are a number of features to note about the Sagrada Familia that distinguish it from other structures, including:
- the structure's organic curves and contours, which are a defining feature of Gaudi's architecture.

- The intricate details found in the church's stained glass windows, mosaics, and sculptures.
- the blending of many styles, such as Gothic and Art Nouveau, to produce a distinctive and eclectic design.

6.Magic Fountain of Montjuic

In the Barcelona area of Montjuic, there is a magnificent show of water, light, and music known as the Magic Fountain of Montjuic. Anyone visiting the city should go to one of the most well-liked attractions there.

History:

Carles Buigas created the Magic Fountain, which was erected in 1929 for the International Exposition. Since being renovated in 1992 for the Olympic Games, the fountain has become a well-liked tourist destination.

Visitor Information:

From Wednesday to Sunday, the public is welcome to visit the Magic Fountain for no charge (hours vary depending on the season). As the area around the fountain can get crowded, it is advised for visitors to arrive early to secure a good viewing spot. For maintenance purposes, the fountain is shut off for the winter.

Tips:

- To get a decent viewing area, arrive early.
- Because the fountain isn't always open, be sure to check the schedule in advance.
- Because the evenings can be chilly, bring a jacket or sweater.
- Respect the fountain's perimeter rules and restrictions by not swimming or climbing on the fountain.

Interesting Things:

- The following are a some of the most intriguing sights and activities at the Magic Fountain:
- The fountain features a magnificent light and water show that is coordinated to music and has a variety of colors and patterns.
- The park in which the fountain is situated: The park is a popular place for picnics and relaxation and gives spectacular views of the city.
- The Montjuic Castle: The neighboring Montjuic Castle provides sweeping views of both the city and the surroundings.

What to Notice:

There are various aspects to note about the Magic Fountain that distinguish it from other attractions, including:

- The fountain's enormous size and ability to shoot water up to a height of 50 meters.
- the art of combining color and light to produce a magnificent visual display.
- The background music, which spans several genres and styles.

7. Guell Park

Entrance: 7€ | **Working hours:** 8 am- 9.30pm (in high season);

On Barcelona's Carmel Hill, Park Guell is a magnificent public park. It is one of the most unique parks in the world, with a mix of architectural, artistic, and natural elements that make it a must-see attraction for visitors to the city.

History:

Built between 1900 and 1914, the park was Antoni Gaudi's creation for rich manufacturer Eusebi Guell. The park was supposed to be a wealthy people's garden city, but the idea was never finished, therefore the city eventually bought the park and made it a public area.

Visitor Information:

Public access to Park Guell is available, and admission is free. The Gaudi House Museum and several of the other attractions in the park, however, have an admission cost. The park is open every day, though the hours of operation change according to the season.

Tips:
- Avoid the crowds by getting there early.
- Due of the park's numerous steep walkways and staircases, wear appropriate footwear.
- Since the park is largely open air and gets very hot in the summer, bring a hat and sunscreen.
- Bring a picnic and take in the lovely city views.

Interesting Things:

Some of the most interesting things to see and do at Park Guell include:

- The park's monumental zone is where you'll find some of Gaudi's most stunning creations, like the dragon fountain, the Hypostyle Room, and the vibrant mosaics.
- The park also has a lovely natural area with wonderful views of the city, a variety of vegetation, and fauna.
- Visitors can tour the home where Gaudi resided for almost 20 years while learning more about his life and work at the Gaudi House Museum.

What to Take Note Of

- Several features that distinguish Park Guell from other parks include the following:
- the park's usage of brilliant mosaics and tiles, which fosters a lively and carefree attitude.
- the characteristically organic curves and contours of Gaudi's building.
- the inclusion of natural components in the park's design, such as rocks and plants

8. Gaudi House Museum

Entry is $5 (4 with the Barcelona Card) and hours are 10 am to 8 pm in the summer and 10 am to 8 pm in the winter (winter)

The Casa Museu Gaudi, also referred to as the Gaudi House Museum, is situated in Barcelona's Park Guell. It is now a museum devoted to the life and work of the renowned architect Antoni Gaudi. It was once his home.

History:

Built in 1904, the Gaudi House Museum was initially intended to serve as a model residence for a housing complex that was being considered for the Park Guell region. Gaudi moved into the residence in 1906, despite the fact that the development was never finished. He stayed there until his death in 1926, and in 1963 it was turned into a museum.

Visitor Information:

The cost of admission to Park Guell includes admission to the Gaudi House Museum, which is open to the public. Learn more about Gaudi's life and work, including how he created Park Guell and other well-known structures in Barcelona, by exploring the museum.

The museum has daily hours that change depending on the season. The cost of entering Park Guell includes admission.

Tips:

- As part of a tour to Park Guell, visit the museum.
- In order to guarantee availability and avoid long waits, buy your tickets in advance.
- To understand more about Gaudi's life and work, think considering joining a museum tour.

Interesting Things:

- As part of a tour to Park Guell, visit the museum.
- In order to guarantee availability and avoid long waits, buy your tickets in advance.
- To understand more about Gaudi's life and work, think considering joining a museum tour.

What to Notice:

The following are a few of the most intriguing sights and activities at the Gaudi House Museum:

- The home's furnishings and decorations give a special glimpse into Gaudi's design aesthetic because they were created by him.
- Aside from his drawings and notes, Gaudi's personal effects are also on display in the museum.
- The residence's breathtaking views of the city and the surroundings are provided by its Park Guell location.

9. Estadi Olímpic Lluís Companys, Palau Sant Jordi, and Olympic Park

8 a.m. to 8 p.m. (summer), 10 a.m. to 6 p.m. (winter)

The stadium was originally constructed in 1927 and refurbished in 1989 for the 1992 Summer Olympics that took place in Barcelona. Several indoor sporting events took place at the Palau Sant Jordi during the 1992 Olympics.

10. Montjuic Castle

Entry: 5 euros 9 a.m. to 9 p.m. (summer), 9 a.m. to 7 p.m. (winter)

It is a historic fortification perched atop a hill overlooking Barcelona. It gives breathtaking views of the surroundings and has a significant place in the history of the city.

History:

- To protect the city from invasion during the Reapers' War, a battle between Catalonia and Spain, the castle was initially constructed in 1640. It has served as a military prison, a place to carry out executions, and a military museum over the years. It is now a well-liked tourist destination and a must-see for anyone traveling to the city.

Visitors' details:

- The Montjuic Castle is accessible to the general public and features guided tours as well as historical exhibits about the city and stronghold. Explore the castle and take in the breathtaking views of the city and surroundings. There is a €5 entrance fee, with elderly and student discounts available.
- Wear comfortable shoes because the castle has a lot of stairwells and steep paths.
- Bring a camera to capture the breathtaking cityscapes.
- To avoid the crowds, go early in the day.
- For information about special events or exhibits, check the schedule.

Among the most fascinating sights and activities in Montjuic Castle are the following:

- The military museum houses displays on the fortress's history as well as Barcelona's military past.

- The castle offers breathtaking panoramic views of the city and its surroundings, including the waterfront and the Mediterranean Sea.
- The castle's architecture is a mash-up of various styles and eras, reflecting its extensive and diverse past.

What to Take Note Of

- There are several features that distinguish the Montjuic Castle from other forts, including:
- The fortress's amazing size, which encompasses numerous buildings and structures over a sizable area.
- the variety of architectural styles, which depict the fortress's long and varied history.
- The castle is a well-liked site for both tourists and locals because of the breathtaking views over the city and the surrounding countryside.

11. Foundation Miro

Entrance: 12€ (free of charge with the Barcelona Card). Barcelona's Montjuic Hill is home to the Joan Miro Foundation, usually referred to as the Fundacio Joan Miro. The museum showcases a sizable collection of paintings, sculptures, and other creations by renowned Catalan artist Joan Miro.

History:

In order to protect and promote his work, the artist himself founded the Joan Miro Foundation in 1975. The museum has a distinctive modernist style that was created by architect Josep Lluis Sert. The museum is currently one of Barcelona's most visited cultural destinations.

Visitor Information:

The public is welcome to visit the Joan Miro Foundation, which also provides guided tours and displays on the artist's life and career. While exploring the museum, visitors can take in breathtaking views of the surrounding area and the city. The entrance charge is €12, with senior and student discounts available.

Tips:

- To prevent any closures or special events, check the museum's schedule in advance.
- To find out more about the artist and his work, think considering going on a tour with a guide.
- Because there are so many ramps and stairs at the museum, wear comfortable shoes.
- Bring a camera to capture the breathtaking cityscapes.

Interesting Things:

Some of the most interesting things to see and do at the Joan Miro Foundation include:

- The museum's permanent collection has more than 14,000 works by Miro, including paintings, sculptures, and prints.
- The museum holds a variety of transient exhibitions all through the year that include the creations of more contemporary artists.
- The museum's outdoor sculpture garden is home to numerous monumental pieces by Miro and other artists.

What to Take Note Of

- There are various aspects of the Joan Miro Foundation that distinguish it from other museums, including:

- Josep Lluis Sert, an architect, was responsible for the museum's unusual modernist architecture.
- The extensive body of Miro's work, which offers a thorough view of the artist's life and career.
- The museum is a well-liked site for both tourists and locals because of the breathtaking views of the city and the surrounding countryside.

The ticket is complimentary if you have the Barcelona card.

11. Barcelona Cathedral

There is no price to enter.

. It is a must-see sight for tourists and one of the most significant religious and cultural landmarks in the city.

History:

Although the cathedral was initially constructed in the 13th century, it has since undergone numerous additions and alterations. it was dedicated in 1339, and the 19th century saw the completion of the Gothic-style front. It continues to play a significant role in Barcelona's religious and cultural life today.

Visitor Information:

Public tours and displays about the cathedral's and the city's past are available at the venue, which is open to the public. It is open for visitors to tour and enjoy, as well as its Gothic architecture, stained glass windows, and other elements. The entrance cost is €7, with senior and student discounts available.

Tips:

- To avoid the crowds, go early in the day.
- Given that it is a religious location, dress accordingly.
- Look over the calendar for services and other events.

Interesting Things:

Some of the most interesting things to see and do at the Barcelona Cathedral include:

- The cathedral's cloister, which features a lovely courtyard and a collection of statues, is a tranquil haven in the middle of the city.
- Stained glass windows: The cathedral has a number of beautiful stained glass windows that add to the interior's vibrant and luminous ambience.
- The rooftop: For breathtaking views of the city and the surroundings, visitors can ascend to the cathedral's rooftop.

What to Notice:

When visiting the Barcelona Cathedral, there are several things to notice that make the cathedral unique, including:

- The pointed arches, ribbed vaults, and flying buttresses that define Gothic architecture.
- The sculpture and art collection, which features pieces by artists including Joan Miro and Pablo Gargallo.
- The combination of religious and cultural influences, which depict Barcelona's lengthy and diverse history.

12. Camp Nou

Entry is 23 euros (21.85 euros with the Barcelona Card) and the museum is open from 9.30 a.m. to 7.30 p.m. during the summer and from 10 a.m. to 6.30 p.m. during the winter.

Barcelona's Les Corts district is home to the renowned Camp Nou football stadium. It is a popular location for football enthusiasts from all over the world and serves as FC Barcelona's home stadium.

Since its debut in 1957, Camp Nou has grown to be among the most recognizable football venues in the world. The stadium has had numerous renovations throughout the years, including a significant upgrade in the 1990s that provided more seating and contemporary amenities. Today, Camp Nou is a must-see location for Barcelona tourists and football fans.

Camp Nou is accessible to the general public and features guided tours, as well as historical exhibitions about the club and the stadium. Visitors are welcome to tour the stadium and its amenities, including the pitch, the press box, and the locker rooms. €30 is the entrance cost, with younger guests and those over 65 paying less.

Tips:

- Because the tour involves a lot of walking, wear comfortable shoes.

- To find out more about the background of the stadium and the team, think about taking a tour.
- Examine the calendar for games and other events.

Interesting Things:

Some of the most interesting things to see and do at Camp Nou include:

- The FC Barcelona Museum has displays on the club's history as well as that of its players, and it is housed inside the stadium.
- The field: Visitors can enter the field and feel what it's like to play football with some of the best players in the world.
- The numerous trophies and honors that FC Barcelona has received, including several Champions League championships, are displayed in the trophy room.

What to Notice:

When visiting Camp Nou, there are several things to notice that make the stadium unique, including:

- the stadium's size, which has a capacity of over 99,000 people.
- the intense atmosphere that permeates games and activities.
- The museum and various exhibits represent the heritage and history of FC Barcelona.

13. Museu d' Historia de la Ciutat

This is Barcelona's city museum and is geared toward fans of ancient history. You enter this spectacular museum through Casa Padellas, a stunning mansion from the sixteenth century. The old Roman city of Barcino, which is located in the museum's underground levels, is then accessible by walking past it. You can find the ruins of the medieval royal residence Placa Del Rei here.

Here are some of the places that you should visit when touring inside this museum:

- Roman funeral way
- Temple of Augustus
- Roman Domus of Saint Honorat
- Villa Joana
- Turo de la Rovira
- Outstaning Catalan Persons Gallery

Address: PLaca del Rei, s/n, Barcelona

Phone:+34 932 56 21 00

14.Museu Barbier-Mueller d'Art Pre-Colombi

This museum specializes in South and Central American pre-Columbian art and cultures. This museum contains a wide variety of priceless South American jewelry. Various statues, fabrics, and pottery are also available.

Address:Carrer de Montcada, 14,Barcelona

Phone:+34 933 10 45 16

15.Museu de la Xocolata

You should check out this museum if you enjoy chocolate. Both young and young at heart can enjoy it. It is also for die-hard chocolate addicts. You may explore the history of chocolate at this museum.

Additionally, you can purchase chocolate replicas of a wide range of subjects, including well-known cartoon characters like Sponge Bob, Tom and Jerry, and Winnie the Pooh, as well as grand tourist attractions like the La Sagrada Familia. Inside "The Chocolate Museum," children will undoubtedly have fun.

Address:Carrer del Comerç, 36,Barcelona

Phone:+34 932 68 78 78

16. Museo del Perfume (Museum of Perfume)

Barcelona offers a wide variety of unique things to do. One of the attractions you must go is the Museum of Perfume. Ancient perfumes from a wide range of cultures are on display in the museum. Although it's tucked away in the back of a large perfume store, this store is still worthwhile visiting.

Address: Passeig de Gràcia, 39,Barcelona

Phone:+34 932 16 01 21

17. Picasso Museum

Few people in the world are unaware of Picasso's existence. He is one of history's finest artists. One of the largest Picasso collections in the world is housed in this museum.

There is no denying that this is Barcelona's most visited art gallery. You should anticipate crowds of people to admire Pablo Picasso's genius if you put his name on something. The Picasso Museum is situated right in the middle of La Ribera.

Five old mansions surround it, giving the area an exquisite, old-world feel that is now relatively uncommon. The treasures that are on show here are beautiful even if you aren't a big fan of art. These are Picasso's more traditional works, which you may see here.

In 1895, Picasso became the first person to set foot on this land. He brought his family along. He quickly built a studio, which at the time was a rather audacious move. If you're interested, the studio is in Carrer de la Plata.

The museum is housed in several important structures, some of which are listed below:

- The first structure the museum has occupied is called Palau Aguilar.
- The palace Palau Meca includes a lovely central courtyard. A multicolored coffered ceiling is also present.
- Palau Finestres: This 1363-built structure is currently being used as an exhibition space.
- Casa Mauri: The Museu Picasso purchased this structure in 1999.

Address: Carrer Montcada, 15-23,Barcelona

Phone:+34 932 56 30 00

18. National Art Museum of Catalonia Barcelona

The first structure the museum has occupied is called Palau Aguilar.

The palace Palau Meca includes a lovely central courtyard. A multicolored coffered ceiling is also present.

Palau Finestres: This 1363-built structure is currently being used as an exhibition space.

Casa Mauri: The Museu Picasso purchased this structure in 1999.

Address: Palau Nacional, Parc de Montjuïc, s/n,Barcelona,

Phone:+34 936 22 03 60

19. Barcelona Museum of Contemporary Art

You must go to this museum during your trip to Barcelona. The extensive items displayed here are quite unique. The museum focuses on three time periods: the 1940s through the 1960s, the 1960s through the 1970s, and the present.

Address: Plaça dels Àngels, 1, 08001 Barcelona

Phone:+34 934 12 08 10

20.Museu Marítim

You will adore what you discover in the Museu Martim if you enjoy gothic art and architecture. There is a Naval Museum there, and the Royal Shipyards are nearby. Collections that attest to Barcelona's illustrious past in the sea can be found here.

The Great Adventure of the Sea is one collection worth mentioning. It is among the more well-liked attractions in this area. It also has small versions of the ships Ferdinand Magellan used to travel across the globe. You can board the Santa Eulàlia, a historic sailing vessel that is currently resting on the Moll de la Fusta, as a way to cap up the journey.

Address:Av. de les Drassanes, s/n,Barcelona

Phone:+34 933 42 99 20

Chapter 4: Itineraries

Enjoy these itineraries for a balanced and enjoyable trip to Barcelona! Adapt or modify as desired. Enjoy!

5-days itinerary

Day 1

Barcelona is a large city, yet it is easily navigable on foot in 5 days. In order to move around town, you can also rent a bike.

When you reach to your hotel (or wherever you're staying), take a moment to unwind, settle in, and then get ready before setting off on your Catalonia adventure. (It's best to get there early.)

Why not start your visit to Barcelona at one of its well-known tourist destinations? Visit the stunning Baslica de la Sagrada Famlia, an imposing Roman Catholic church built in 1882 by renowned Catalan architect Antoni Gaud with elements of Gothic and Art Nouveau.

We strongly advise visiting this church from the outside, even if you decide not to go inside (there is frequently a big line!). Since 1882, work has been ongoing because to numerous financial setbacks, civil conflicts, and other factors. Unbelievable, no?

If you're still hungry after that, stop by the nearby La Taqueria Mexican restaurant for some food! Although the pricing are tourist-driven due to the location, the tacos here are some of the best in Barcelona!

There is also a lot more Antoni Gaud to see around the city after lunch. After witnessing the Basilica de la Sagrada Familia, you will be able to recognize Gaud's work wherever you are, even if you have no background in architecture or art.

Next, we advise seeing Casa Vicens, his first major construction, which was completed in 1888 for a well-to-do local family. It's in Barcelona's Grácia district, and in our opinion, it deserves much more attention.

A must-see is La Pedrera (Casa Milá), Gaud's final piece of architecture. More sculpture than building, really.

After a long day of travel and taking in today's first sights, you're undoubtedly exhausted, so we advise eating dinner at your hotel or at a nearby restaurant before retiring for a restful night. Tomorrow is coming!

Location Information

Basillica de la Sagrada Família

Address: Carrer de Mallorca, 401, 08013, Barcelona, Spain

Tel: +34 935 132 060

http://www.sagradafamilia.org/en

La Taqueria (Restaurant)

Address: Passatge de Font, 5, 08013, Barcelona, Spain

Tel: +34 931 261 359

http://www.lataqueria.eu

Casa Vicens

Address: Carrer de les Carolines, 18-24, 08012, Barcelona, Spain

http://www.casavicens.es

La Pedrera

Address: Provença, 261-265, 08008, Barcelona, Spain

Tel: +34 902 202 138

https://www.lapedrera.com/en/home

Day 2

Set out for Parc Güell, one of Barcelona's most renowned landmarks, after a leisurely breakfast at your hotel! This geometric park was created by Antoni Gaud between 1900 and 1914, and it is now a UNESCO World Heritage Site. On Carmel Hill, there is a special garden complex that contains a number of intriguing architectural buildings. Including Gaudí's own home, now the **Gaudí House Museum**: http://www.casamuseugaudi.org/cm-eng

For lunch, We advise visiting the close-by Maigot Café. Delicious sandwiches, pizzas, and salads are available here, and everyone is quite welcoming.

From there, proceed to Palau Güell, another one of Gaud's masterpieces that served as industrial billionaire Eusebi Güell's private mansion. It served as the backdrop for the 1975 Jack Nicholson and Maria Schneider movie The Passenger.

Camp Nou, home to the renowned soccer team Futbol Club Barcelona (Barça), is yet another must-see tourist destination in Barcelona. The second-biggest football stadium in the world by capacity is Camp Nou, which is also the largest stadium in Europe.

And if you're a football enthusiast (or traveling with one), you must explore the FCB Musuem at Camp Nou. The view of the stadium from the gallery is a standout highlight; it is breathtaking!

Visit Barcelona's largest, oldest, and best market, La Boqueria (Mercat de Sant Josep de la Boqueria), if you have time this evening. The covered sections were first used around 1840, although the open-air locations were first used for the sale of meat in the Middle Ages. There are stores where you can buy apparel, souvenirs, and, of course, some of the best food Spain has to offer.

If this fits you, you can get a picnic-style dinner here; otherwise, go to El Quim de la Boqueria! El Quim, located right in La Boqueria, offers delectable seafood and tapas, a Spanish meal must!

Location Information

Parc Güell

Address: Carrer d'Olot, s/n, 08024, Barcelona, Spain

Tel: +34 902 200 302

http://www.parkguell.cat/en

Palau Güell

Address: Carrer Nou de la Rambla, 3-5, 08001, Barcelona, Spain

Tel: +34 934 725 775

http://palauguell.cat/en

Maigot Café

Address: Carrer de la Mare de Déu del Coll, 71, 08023, Barcelona, Spain

Phone Number: +34 932 101 223

Camp Nou & FCB Museum

Address: Avinguda Aristides Maillol, 12, 08028, Barcelona, Spain

Tel: +34 902 189 900

Main Website:

http://www.fcbarcelona.com/camp-nou

FCB Museum Website:

http://www.fcbarcelona.com/camp-nou/detail/card/fcb-museum

La Boqueria

Address: Plaza de la Boqueria | Ramblas, 08001, Barcelona, Spain

Tel: +34 933 18 25 84

http://www.boqueria.info/index.php?lang=en

El Quim de la Boqueria

Address: Mercado de La Boqueria, Les Rambles, 91, 08002, Barcelona, Spain

Tel: +34 933 019 810

http://elquimdelaboqueria.cat

Day 3

Would you like to go to the beach today? Beach (in Spanish, "playa"; in Catalan, "platja") Take a quick train to Nova Icaria Beach for a fantastic day of outdoor recreation! This beach is one of our favorites since it's calm and offers a ton of services, including free Wi-Fi, showers, table tennis, volleyball, assistance for disabled beachgoers, a kids' section, and more. You can also bring a picnic basket from the market or eat lunch or dinner at one of the many excellent restaurants in the area.

From here, you can easily access the Icária shopping area, where a VO (Version Originale) theater that screens movies in their original languages is located. There are many English-language movies. So, you can visit Yelmo Icària Cinema after a fun day at the beach.

Barceloneta Beach is the most well-known of Barcelona's beaches, however there are many people there and, in our opinion, it's not as clean as other beaches. We wouldn't choose it; it's not one of our favorites.

If you're interested, there is a nudist beach in Barcelona. In Barcelona, only La Mar Bella Beach is recognized as a nudist beach. (Postal code: 08019 Passeig de Garcia Faria, Barcelona, Spain)

We suggest the city's top restaurant, Petit Pau, for dinner today. In our opinion, they serve some of Spain's best steaks and seafood.

Location Information

Platja de la Nova Icária (Beach)

Address: Passeig Marítim de Nova Icària, 08005, Barcelona, Spain

Tel: +34 932 85 38 34

Yelmo Icària Cinema

Address: Calle Salvador Espiriu, 61, El Centre de la Vila, Port Olimpic, 08005, Barcelona, Spain

Tel: +34 932 217 585

http://www.yelmocines.es/cine/yelmo-cines-icaria

Viator (Mediterranean Boat Tour)

Tel: 1-888-651-9785

http://www.viator.com/tours/Barcelona/Private-Tour-Barcelona-Sailing-Trip/d562-5571PARTYSAIL

Runner Bean Tours Barcelona

Address: Carrer del Carme 44, pral 2ª 08001, Barcelona, Spain

Tel: +34 636 108 776

http://www.runnerbeantours.com/barcelona-tours/walking-tour-kids-y-family/7

Petit Pau Restaurant

Address: Carrer de l'Espanya Industrial, 22, 08014, Barcelona, Spain

Tel: +34 933 313 275

https://www.facebook.com/pages/Petit-Pau-Restaurant/234136820076860

Day 4

Time for a day trip! It's time to short depart Barcelona so you may see the renowned Montserrat Mountains. The Montserrat and Cava Trail Viator tour is highly recommended since it offers excellent value and a memorable experience, including short treks, delectable meals, and wine tastings. Enjoy the final day!

Viator

Tel: 1-888-651-9785

http://www.viator.com/tours/Barcelona/Montserrat-and-Cava-Trail-Small-Group-Day-Trip-from-Barcelona/d562-3142MONT

Day 5

Since you've just returned from a day excursion, today can be laid-back and unstructured with free time, or you can get out and about with the full day of new adventures we've planned for you below!

Don't miss Las Ramblas, Barcelona's busiest, most well-known, tree-lined street, after a leisurely, leisurely breakfast at your hotel (or streets rather, there are five of them). It's a bustling open pedestrian mall with a unique local flavor where everything is occurring. It's a wonderful area to spend your fifth day, meandering through in the morning before the afternoon crowds arrive. It is cobblestoned and flanked with lovely trees. Las Ramblas is the best area to go shopping if you're seeking for fantastic stores!

Don't forget to visit the Christopher Columbus statue, which is located at the southern end of the main street. From here, you can also see Port Vell, a harbor on the water and a historic port in Barcelona.

One word of advice: be on the lookout for pickpockets around the Las Rambla neighborhood. Keep your bags and purse in a secure place, and it's advisable to avoid carrying anything valuable in your back pocket, like your phone, wallet, or wallet.

You should go to Elisabets for lunch. We consider it to have a hip ambiance and to be just far enough from a "tourist trap" to be a fantastic place to enjoy regional food like tapas, Mediterranean sandwiches, and more.

Barcelona's Gothic Quarter is located to the east of Las Ramblas (Barri Gotic) This pedestrian area is a must-see because of the maze-like street layout, which offers plenty of Kodak opportunity!

Next, you can travel to the Museu Picasso (The Picasso Museum), which has one of the largest and most comprehensive collections of Pablo Picasso's works of art. Here, Picasso's remarkable connection to Barcelona is exemplified and preserved in exquisite fashion.

Don't forget to eat at the adjacent Taperia Princesa this evening! Fast, delectable Spanish and Mediterranean cuisine served in a pleasant setting. Enjoy a great sangria while you can!

You might perhaps attend an outdoor movie showing if you're searching for something to do this evening. The majority of the time, the weather in Barcelona is ideal for outdoor cinema viewing, and during the past few years, more and more film festivals have been held there. The Sala Montjuc is one of the places to see movies; it also hosts concerts and gives tours of the Montjuc Castle. Tickets and showtimes can be found on their website in advance.

Location Information

Las Ramblas (Shopping District)

Address: La Rambla, Ciutat Vella, 08002, Barcelona, Spain

http://www.barcelonaturisme.com/wv3/en/page/160/la-rambla.html

Elisabets (Restaurant)

Address: Carrer d'Elisabets, 2-4, 08001, Barcelona, Spain

Tel: +34 933 175 826

http://www.tripadvisor.com/Restaurant_Review-g187497-d693967-Reviews-Elisabets-Barcelona_Catalonia.html

Gothic Quarter, Barcelona

Address: Mediterranean Seafront to Ronda de Sant Pere, Ciutat Vella, 08002, Barcelona, Spain

http://www.tripadvisor.com/Attraction_Review-g187497-d190162-Reviews-Gothic_Quarter_Barri_Gotic-Barcelona_Catalonia.html

Museo Picasso

Address: Carrer de Montcada, 15-23, 08003, Barcelona, Spain

Tel: +34 932 563 000

http://www.museupicasso.bcn.cat/en

Taperia Princesa

Address: Carrer de la Princesa, 20, 08003, Barcelona, Spain

Tel: +34 632 272 392

http://www.tripadvisor.com/Restaurant_Review-g187497-d2547681-Reviews-Taperia_Princesa-Barcelona_Catalonia.html

Sala Montjuïc (Open-Air Cinema)

Address: Carretera de Montjuic, 66, Barcelona, Spain

Tel: +34 933 023 553

http://salamontjuic.org/en

3-DAY ITINERARY

Day 1:

- Visit the majestic basilica known as the Sagrada Familia to start your day off well. It was created by renowned architect Antoni Gaudi.
- Next, visit the Gothic Quarter to stroll around the quaint plazas and winding streets. Don't forget to visit the magnificent, 13th-century Barcelona Cathedral.
- After lunch, go down Las Ramblas, a busy boulevard lined with stores, eateries, and street performers.
- Go to the beach in the evening to unwind and take in the sunset.

Day 2:

- Spend the morning at Park Guell, a whimsical Gaudi-designed park that provides breathtaking city vistas.
- Visit the Picasso Museum in the afternoon to view a vast collection of the artist's creations, many of which date to his formative years in Barcelona.
- Visit the hip El Raval district for dinner and sample some regional tapas.

Day 3:

Visit the Montjuic Castle first thing in the morning for awe-inspiring views of the city and the port.

Next, proceed to the spectacular music venue Llus Domènech I Montaner's Palau de la Musica Catalana, which was built in the modernist architectural style.

Take a stroll through the Poble Espanyol, a distinctive outdoor museum that displays the variety of Spain's regions, in the afternoon.

7-DAY ITINERARY

Day 1:

- Pay a visit to the renowned Sagrada Familia first thing in the morning. Admire the amazing architecture of Antoni Gaud while exploring the spectacular basilica's interior.
- After that, visit Park Güell, another masterpiece by Gaud. Take a leisurely stroll through the park, take in the mosaics' vibrant colors, and enjoy the expansive vistas of Barcelona.
- Sit down for a quick meal at one of the neighboring cafés.
- Investigate Barri Gtic's ancient area (Gothic Quarter). Explore the Gothic Cathedral, get lost

- in the maze-like streets, and find hidden jewels like Plaça Reial and Plaça Sant Felip Neri.
- The most well-known market in Barcelona is La Boqueria. Enjoy the lively ambiance while sampling some delectable regional fare.
- For dinner, visit the energetic district of El Raval. Choose from a wide selection of international food alternatives while taking in the area's thriving nightlife.
- At Barceloneta Beach, take a leisurely stroll down the boardwalk to unwind before the sun sets.

Day 2:

- Visit Park de la Ciutadella to begin your day. Take in the tranquility, rent a rowboat on the lake, and explore the stunning Cascada Monumental.
- Visit the neighboring Picasso Museum after a brief stroll. Investigate Pablo Picasso's vast body of work to learn more about the artist's life.
- Go to El Born, an upscale area. Explore quaint streets that are home to upscale cafes, boutique stores, and art galleries.
- Experience the majestic Gothic architecture of the Santa Maria del Mar church.
- At one of El Born's neighborhood pubs, savor a fantastic tapas meal.
- Take a trip around the bustling Passeig de Gràcia street. Admire the modernist structures, such as Casa Milà and Casa Batlló (La Pedrera).
- Enjoy a gourmet dining experience at one of the city's restaurants with a Michelin star.

Day 3:

- the early morning Visit the Montjuc Hill area. For breathtaking views of the city, start by going to

Montjuc Castle. Discover the Magic Fountain and the Olympic Stadium as you explore Montjuc Park.
- Sunday afternoon Visit FC Barcelona's home field, the renowned Camp Nou Stadium. Learn about the club's heritage and passion for football by taking a tour of the stadium and museum.
- Take advantage of a late lunch at one of the neighborhood eateries.
- Investigate the thriving Gràcia area. Explore the lovely plazas, meander through the winding streets, and take in the bohemian vibe.
- Visit a neighborhood bar in the evening for a drink and some live music.

Day 4:

- Visit the magnificent Montserrat Monastery, which is about an hour west of Barcelona, on a day excursion. Due to the monastery's magnificent location and breathtaking views of the surrounding mountains, this is one of the most well-liked day trips from Barcelona.

Day 5:

- Visit the Barcelona Museum of Contemporary Art, the National Art Museum of Catalonia, and the Joan Miro Foundation during your day of museum hopping in the city.
- Visit the hip Born neighborhood in the evening to sample some of the greatest artisan drinks in the area.

Day 6:

- Visit the lovely town of Girona for the day, which is about an hour's drive north of Barcelona. This charming town is well-known for its magnificent cathedral and medieval buildings.

Day 7:

- Explore the city's many parks, including as the lovely Ciutadella Park and the Parc de la Creueta del Coll, during the day.
- The best vegetarian and vegan food in the city can be found in the Gracia area, therefore visit there in the evening.

14-DAYS ITINERARY

Day 1:

- Visit the famous Sagrada Familia, an architectural marvel by Antoni Gaudi, to begin your journey. Explore the interior of this magnificent church and take in its exquisite features.
- After that, take a leisurely stroll down Passeig de Gracia, which is renowned for its posh boutiques and striking modernist buildings. Two of Gaudi's architectural masterpieces, Casa Batlló and Casa Milà, must not be missed.

Day 2:

- Explore the Gothic Quarter (Barri Gtic) in the morning. Explore the Barcelona Cathedral, its winding lanes, hidden squares, and its antique structures.
- Visit the Picasso Museum in the afternoon. It is home to a sizable collection of the famed artist's works, many of which date back to his formative years.

Day 3:

- Visit Montserrat, a stunning mountain range and place of spiritual solace, on a day excursion. Visit the Montserrat Monastery, take a ride on the funicular for sweeping views, and go trekking amid breathtaking natural scenery.

Day 4:

- Take in the lively ambiance of La Boqueria Market, one of the biggest food marketplaces in Europe. Discover its vibrant markets, indulge in regional specialties, and purchase fresh ingredients for a picnic.
- Go to Park Guell in the afternoon and stroll around its fascinating gardens, which feature some of Gaudi's most distinctive architectural creations.

Day 5:

- Investigate the hip El Raval neighborhood. Admire the collection of modern art at the Contemporary Art Museum of Barcelona (MACBA) before exploring the nearby Raval Quarter, which is renowned for its vibrant streets and ethnic environment.

Day 6:

- Visit Sitges for the day; it's a quaint seaside town renowned for its lovely beaches and active LGBT community. Explore the town's artistic and cultural heritage while lounging on the beach and strolling along the promenade.

Day 7:

- Explore the Hospital de Sant Pau, a modernist structure created by Llus Domènech I Montaner, and its architectural marvels. Explore the calming grounds and colorful pavilions.

- Visit Barcelona's largest park, Park de la Ciutadella, in the afternoon. Explore the zoo, rent a rowboat for the lake, or just unwind amidst the lovely vegetation.

Day 8:

- Discover the thriving Gracia area, which is renowned for its artistic and independent stores. Explore its quaint squares, like Plaça del Sol and Plaça de la Vila de Gracia, and dine at one of the many restaurants there to sample regional food.

Day 9:

- Visit the Salvador Dali Theatre-Museum in Figueres for the day. It is a tribute to the surrealist artist. Get lost in his imaginative universe by exploring his amazing works.

Day 10:

- Explore the Forum area's cutting-edge architecture. Check out the spectacular Forum Building, take a stroll along the coastal promenade, and unwind at Bogatell Beach, which is close by.

Day 11:

- Visit the MNAC to see its vast collection of Romanesque, Gothic, Renaissance, and contemporary artwork. The terrace of the museum offers breathtaking views of Barcelona, so don't miss it.

Day 12:

- Discover the lovely Poble-Sec neighborhood. At the city's numerous local taverns and eateries, savor mouthwatering tapas and traditional Catalan food. After that, attend a performance at the venerable El Molino theater.

Day 13:

- Pedal around Barcelona's numerous neighborhoods, parks, and landmarks as you begin a bike tour. This is a fantastic opportunity to travel further and experience the city from a new angle.

Day 14:

Spend your final day at leisure, visiting familiar locations or discovering new ones.

Chapter 5:
Where To Stay in Barcelona

We Boutique Hotel

The well-known painter Josep Maria Sert once resided in the building where this charming hotel is now housed. Salvador Dal was a friend of Josep Maria Sert, a well-known artist. Both the We Boutique Hotel's elegance and location are excellent. The motel is cozy and offers excellent service because it only has six rooms.

Address:2a, Ronda de Sant Pere, 70, Barcelona

Phone:+34 932 50 39 91

Casa Bella Gracia

This nice budget hotel is away from all the crowds of Barcelona and will give you a cosy hideout when visiting Barcelona. The position in the Gracia town will make you feel like you're in old-school Barcelona with its charming ambiance and narrow streets. The Casa Bella Gracia is a cutting-edge hotel with a welcoming atmosphere. The hotel only has 12 rooms and has a lovely roof terrace for having a cup of coffee or breakfast.

Address:Carrer de Sant Agustí, 4, Barcelona

Phone:+34 638 49 34 28

Praktik Bakery, Eixample Dreta

A hotel and bakery have partnered to create the novel hotel idea known as Praktik Bakery Hotel in Barcelona. The bakery is on the ground floor, while the rooms are on the higher stories. The amazing part is that you can just go downstairs and grab a coffee and fantastic fresh bread. Although the rooms are not very huge, they have everything you need.

Address:Carrer de Provença, 279,Barcelona

Phone:+34 934 88 00 61

Hotel Ciutat De Barcelona

The lovely Born neighborhood is where the Hotel Ciutat De Barcelona is situated. Despite its simplicity, this hotel offers excellent service and a lovely rooftop terrace with a pool. This is a great value for a cheap hotel, plus it's in one of Barcelona's greatest districts..

Address: Carrer de la Princesa, 33 - 35, Barcelona

Phone:+34 932 69 74 75

Hotel Pulitzer

If you want to stay in the center of Barcelona and don't mind the crowds, this is a good hotel. The hotel is wonderful and will offer you a tranquil getaway from Barcelona's busy streets, despite the area's reputation as a party district. You may unwind in the hotel's elegant lobby on white leather sofas after a long day of touring Barcelona.

Address: Carrer de Bergara, 8,Barcelona

Phone:+34 934 81 67 67

Chapter 6:
Catalan Cuisine

Food from Catalonia has strong ties to other parts of Spain, particularly Valencia and the Balearic Islands, as well as the south, where many workers from Andalusia and Extremadura arrived in the 20th century. It's not just a matter of a few localized specialties, although the region has a reputation for producing some of Spain's best cuisine; rather, it has a gastronomy that is unique from that of the rest of the nation or of nearby France. Despite its varied geography, Catalonia produces a wide range of fresh, premium meat, poultry, game, fruit, and vegetables. These can be prepared in odd combinations, such as fish and nuts, chicken and fruit, or beef and seafood (mar I muntanya, the local version of surf 'n' turf).

Barcelona and the neighboring territories have gained a reputation for their cuisine and dining traditions on a global scale. The region has gained worldwide recognition in recent years thanks to the new generation of innovative chefs in the field of gastronomy, including

Ferran Adria. However, Catalunya has long been a destination that foodies must visit.

Fuets and butifarras are popular pork sausages in Catalonia, but unlike chorizo, they do not contain paprika. They also enjoy garlic, and they utilize it to create their most recognizable sauces, romesco and aioli, which is Catalan for "garlic and oil." They handle vegetables in fairly unusual ways, such as by burning the skins to give them a smokey flavor, as in escalivada, or by using the peels to thicken sauces in fish or meat stews. Although a "picada" (a mixture of almonds, parsley, and garlic) is added towards the conclusion of cooking, flour is rarely actually used. They also created pa amb tomàquet, which is toasted bread that has been rubbed with fresh, ripe tomato, garlic, salt, and olive oil. This is one of my favorite snacks.

Catalan cuisine offers an incredible variety. There is a huge range of foods to sample in Catalan cuisine. Pa amb tomàquet, calçots, and escalivada are a few examples of classic vegetarian Catalan cuisine. Baby leeks are grilled and then served with romesco sauce as calçots. This meal is only served in the spring. Escalivada is a warm side dish made with grilled vegetables that have been peeled, seeded, and served with oil. Typically, it contains aubergines, red peppers, onions, and tomatoes.

If you enjoy beef, give butifarra a try. Similar to Cumberland sausage, butifarra is a red-spiced sausage. Escudellla, a Catalan stew cooked with a piece of meat, beans, potatoes, cabbage, and occasionally pasta, is another fantastic meat meal. Literally meaning "lamb roasted with 12 heads of garlic," Xai Rostit Amb 12 Cabeçes d'All describes what they provide. A platter of cured meats, containing jamon from the Vic region and fuet (pig), is known as a "embutidos."

You must try the fish dishes esqueixada, fideuas, and suquet de peix. Red wine vinegar, shredded "bacalao," peppers, tomatoes, onions, and other ingredients are used to make escqueixada. Cod that has been preserved in salt and is soaked before serving is called balao and is typical of this area. Similar to seafood paella, fideuas is served with short noodles as opposed to rice. A fish stew called suquet de peix includes tomato, potatoes, and garlic. Depending on what has been caught that day, a variety of fish can be utilized in the stew.

Excellent sweets are another hallmark of Catalan cuisine. While visiting Barcelona, I highly recommend trying crema catalana. It resembles crème brulée from France. Sugar, egg yolks, cinnamon, and a burnt top are the main ingredients. Mel I Mato is a mild, unsalted goat cheese that is typically served with honey and walnuts. Small, circular candies called panellets are created from almonds, sugar, eggs, and pine nuts. They can be covered in a variety of coatings, although pine nuts are the most common one. Music is another wonderful thing to explore. It is served with a glass of sweet muscatel wine and consists of dried fruits and nuts that are occasionally combined with ice cream or cream cheese.

Chapter 7: Where to Eat in Barcelona?

In Spain, the menu will include a list of every item. Keep in mind that nothing on the menu may be changed, and rarely can you add your own courses (or add another course to your meals).

The majority of the restaurants will close at 4 pm and reopen at 8 pm, which is a crucial fact to keep in mind. The owners of shops and restaurants typically take their naps in the afternoon. If you don't want to go hungry at those periods, you should get a portable snack.

However, several international franchises and other regional eateries do serve tourists during siesta. Make a mental note of the location if you come across one along the road, or even better, note it down in your schedule. You can return to the restaurant and eat a full dinner if you grow hungry while exploring the city's various attractions.

What Dishes do they Serve?

Don't worry if fish appears in a lot of the foods you'll be served. Expect Mediterranean cuisine because you're in the region. You are getting a healthy dinner for your money because it does have a good mixture of fruits and vegetables.

However, you should be aware that this seafood isn't particularly regional. When you convert an entire city to tourism, that's another setback. Tapas, which are frequently offered in bars as well, are among the specialties of the regional cuisine.

Although not a particularly healthy serving of meat, it is unquestionably flavorful. Be prepared to spend more money for something that tastes nice because it is unfortunately not cheap. You'll also see that there are many of street vendors selling waffles here.

You will have to learn this information on your own because the majority of tour guides won't divulge it to you. Try the waffles offered here if you enjoy them. Compared to the Belgian waffles that most people are used to, they make a good startling contrast. They taste exactly as nice as they smell, in fact.

So How Much Do I Pay for a Meal?

Anywhere in the world, food prices will inevitably change. Whether you are in Barcelona or not is irrelevant. To give you a general idea, a one-person budget supper in this city will likely cost around 10 Euros. An average supper for one person (with a drink) can cost up to 25 euros. Spending more money on food (above 25 euros) is referred to as overspending.

Where to Find the Good Restaurants?

The best eateries are spread all over Barcelona. However, there are some locations where you can find large groups of eateries, bars, and restaurants serving delectable meals.

Barceloneta

Barceloneta is one region that is well-liked by both tourists and locals. Here you'll find some of the best examples of the regional baked fish dish if you've grown to love it. Locally, the dish is referred to as paella. Arrs negre, a serving of black rice, is another well-known local delicacy.

The top-notch restaurants can be found in different parts of the city. Eixample Esquerra, which is situated halfway between Gran Via and the well-known Mallorca, is among those places. You might wish to try one of the many eateries in Plaça Catalunya. El Born, which lies nearby Barri Gtic and is a fantastic site to try the local cuisine, is yet another interesting location to visit.

- Eixample Esquerra
- Plaça Catalunya
- El Born
- Barri Gòtic

Restaurants

Can Costa

Can Costa is one restaurant you might wish to try since we've previously mentioned Barceloneta. This is where you might find your heart's content if you love seafood. The location is along Passeig de Joan de Borbón, which is not very difficult to find.

If you get lost, just search for the waterfront and proceed to walk back one block to find Can Costa. It's not all that difficult to locate. One thing you should know is that locals typically eat here, so keep that in mind. You already know all you need to know about this restaurant from this.

Try fideuà de paella, one of their highly recommended dishes, if you enjoy trying the local cuisine. Yes, it's another fish dish that has been baked, but don't be discouraged. This is the authentic baked fish meal from Catalonia, if you're yearning to try it. You'll notice that this recipe uses noodles rather than rice.

Tiny calamari should be ordered if you can't get enough of the seafood offered here. That is breaded and fried squid. Remember that if you don't get here before 2 pm, you won't be able to get a table. Due to the venue's high popularity, reservations are not always possible.

Address:Passeig de Joan de Borbó, 70

Phone:+34 932 21 59 03

Bar Marsella

Bar Marsella is another renowned dining establishment. The address is 65 Carrer Sant Pau. This is yet another excellent location to find authentic Catalan cuisine. You'll like the decor as well. The majority of it dates back to the 19th century, as seen by the rafters, extremely ornate heavy draperies, and high ceiling-mounted chandeliers.

To get here take the subway to Liceu Metro.

Address:Carrer de Sant Pau, 65

Phone:+34 934 42 72 63

Set Portes

This establishment serves seafood and traditional paella. This location, which has existed in Barcelona since 1836, has a fantastic vibe. Amazing meals may be found here.

Take the subway to Metro Barceloneta to get here.

Address:Passeig Isabel II, 14,

Phone:+34 933 19 30 33

Can Culleretes

One of Spain's oldest eateries, Can Culleretes, has been operating since 1786. Delicious meal and a wonderful atmosphere. Various typical Spanish cuisine are available.

Take the subway to Metro Liceu to get there.

Address:Carrer d'en Quintana, 5

Phone:+34 933 17 30 22

Chapter 8:
Barcelona Nightlife, Entertainment and souvenirs.

Barcelona is renowned for its exciting nightlife, which provides a variety of entertainment alternatives to suit all tastes. There is usually something going on in the city after sundown, from bustling bars and clubs to secluded live music places and cultural shows..

Bars and Clubs

Whether you're searching for a laid-back cocktail bar, an energetic dance club, or a secret speakeasy, the city's varied bar and club scene has something to offer everyone. areas and venues with a thriving nightlife include:

1. **El Raval:** This diverse area is home to a wide range of bars and clubs, providing everything from chill hangouts to energetic dance clubs. Marsella, a venerable absinthe bar, and Macarena Club, a modest but energetic dance club, are notable locations.
2. **The old Gothic Quarter** is home to a variety of bars and clubs, many of which are tucked away

in the winding lanes and little passageways. Be sure to check out Pipa Club, a welcoming and distinctive club concealed inside a residential property, as well as Ocaa, a chic bar and restaurant with a gorgeous terrace.
3. **Poble Sec:** With a number of hip bars and clubs, this emerging neighborhood is swiftly developing a reputation as a hub for nightlife. Don't forget to visit Sala Apolo, a renowned club and live music venue, as well as the well-known Carrer Blai, a pedestrian boulevard dotted with bustling bars and tapas joints.
4. **Port Olmpic:** Offering a glam night out with breathtaking ocean views, the waterfront district of Port Olmpic is well-known for its luxury clubs and beachfront bars. Famous clubs like Pacha, Shôko, and Opium draw both residents and visitors looking for a fun night of dancing.

Live Music and Cultural Performances

The live music and culture scene in Barcelona is vibrant and eclectic, featuring everything from classic flamenco performances to contemporary electronic music. Popular locations and occasions include:

1. **Gran Teatre del Liceu**: Numerous performances are held at this historic opera theatre on La Rambla, including opera, ballet, and concerts of classical music. It is a must-visit cultural attraction because of its magnificent architecture and extensive history. https://www.liceubarcelona.cat
2. **Palau de la Música Catalana**: This Llus Domènech I Montaner-designed modernist music hall is a masterpiece of architecture and a UNESCO World Heritage Site. The location

presents a variety of events and performances, including jazz, world music, and classical music.
3. **Razzmatazz**: Razzmatazz, one of the most recognizable live music venues in the city, features a broad roster of both national and local performers, ranging from electronic DJs to indie bands. The multi-room facility welcomes music enthusiasts of all genres with its distinctive and energetic environment .https://www.salarazzmatazz.com
4. **Tablao Flamenco Cordobes**: Visit Tablao Flamenco Cordobes in La Rambla for a genuine flamenco experience. Some of the top flamenco performers in the nation perform weekly in this quaint setting, offering a passionate and unforgettable cultural experience.

Festivals and Events

Barcelona holds a number of festivals and events all year long to honor the city's rich traditions, history, and culture. Visitors have a special chance to take in the lively ambiance of the city and take in a variety of entertainment at these events. Festivals and events that are well-liked include:

1. **Festa Major de Gràcia**: The streets of Gràcia are turned into vibrant, themed displays during this annual street festival, which lasts for a whole week in August and features live music, food vendors, and cultural events. It's a lively and authentic celebration of local culture. https://www.festamajordegracia.cat
2. **La Mercè**: Every year in August, the streets of Gràcia are transformed into vibrant, themed displays, with live music, food stalls, and cultural activities.human tower building (castellers), and

fireworks displays.
https://www.barcelona.cat/lamerce
3. **Primavera Sound**: This yearly music festival, which takes place in late May or early June, draws an impressive lineup of artists from all genres, both local and foreign. The festival, which takes place at the Parc del Frum, provides music fans with a variety of stages and a lively environment.
4. **Sónar Festival**: Sónar is a cutting-edge electronic music and digital arts event that takes place in June. Renowned DJs, producers, and multimedia artists play there. The festival is split into Sónar by Day and Sónar by Night, providing participants with a distinctive and immersive experience. https://sonar.es

Family-Friendly Entertainment

Families may enjoy a variety of family-friendly entertainment alternatives in Barcelona, which makes it possible for travelers of all ages to take advantage of the city's energetic environment and varied attractions. Several well-liked options for family entertainment include:

1. **Parc de la Ciutadella**: With its abundance of amenities, including a boating lake, playgrounds, and the Barcelona Zoo, this park is a favorite among families. Throughout the year, the park also hosts a number of festivals and cultural events.
2. **Tibidabo Amusement Park**: This old amusement park, located on the Tibidabo Mountain, has a variety of rides and activities for visitors of all ages as well as stunning views of the city below. https://www.tibidabo.cat

3. **L'Aquàrium Barcelona**: A wide variety of marine life, including sharks, rays, and penguins, can be found at this sizable aquarium, which is situated in the Port Vell region. With its engaging exhibits and interactive experiences, it's a popular destination for families.
https://www.aquariumbcn.com
4. **CosmoCaixa**: The science museum in Barcelona is a fascinating and instructive place for families because it features a variety of interactive exhibits and hands-on activities. Highlights include the planetarium, the tropical rainforest exhibit, and the geological wall.
https://www.cosmocaixa.es

Explore the Explosive Nightlife in Barcelona

Just like the city itself, the stunning Catalan nightlife is easily characterized as spectacular and diverse. Therefore, be sure to explore this lovely location at night when you go there. Here are some great locations in Barcelona where you can get a taste of the vibrant Catalan nightlife.

Enjoy a Latin-themed evening at Mojito Club.

Learn how to salsa dance if you want to truly enjoy Barcelona's nightlife, and Mojito Club, the locals' favorite club, is the ideal setting for a sensuous salsa dancing affair.

Travelers who are committed to participating in this must overcome their customary reluctance and begin dancing, especially if they want to benefit from the salsa lessons the club gives at 10 p.m. After midnight, the salsa bar transforms into a nightclub, but the authentic Latin and Cuban vibes last right up to the end of the party. This allows everyone to continue dancing till sunrise while displaying their daring moves.

Razzmatazz offers a complete clubbing experience in Barcelona.

If you want to have the best nightlife experience possible, you should be at Razzmatazz, one of Barcelona's most well-known clubs. The club is organized into five distinct rooms, each of which offers a distinctive ambience and, of course, various musical genres.

Razzmatazz is the place for you if you want to dance while listening to the newest techno music or just want to move your body while listening to the hottest "Top 20 Hits."

Razzmatazz Phone: 933 20 82 00 Address: Carrer dels Almogàvers, 122, 08018 Barcelona| Hours: Wednesday: 11:59PM-5AM, | Friday&Saturday: 11:59PM-6AM

Don't Miss Port Olympic's Upscale Experience

Travelers can spend their evenings exploring Port Olympic if they desire to experience Catalan nightlife in a more upscale setting. The finest location for summer parties is here, however many clubs are open year-round.

Before entering the clubs and getting into the swing of things, people frequently have a few enticing cocktails on one of the upscale beach terraces. Most of these establishments close at 3 a.m., unlike other clubs in Barcelona. Some, like Opium and Pacha, stay open until six in the morning. As a result, there are several clubs to select from if you wish to attend a party in the Port Olympic area. The best part is that you can always head to the beach and unwind for a while if you start to feel overstimulated by the hectic atmosphere inside the clubs.

Opium Barcelona is located in Passeig Martim, 34, in Barcelona and is open from 12 p.m. until 6 a.m.

Pacha Barcelona Phone Number: 932 21 56 28 Address: Passeig Martim Barceloneta, 38, 08003 Barcelona

Embrace a Stylish Setting and Delight in a Delectable Cocktail

Although there are many venues in Barcelona where lovers of the drink can indulge in the most peculiar concoctions, Dry Martini is unquestionably one of the greatest. This is especially true if you want to experience the sophisticated side of Catalonian nightlife.

When you first go into Dry Martini, you might start to feel as though you've traveled back in time, but as soon as you try one of the amazing drinks made by the classic barmen dressed in swanky tuxedos, you realize that you are in the present, and you adore it. There is undoubtedly no better way to spend a night out in Barcelona if you don't want to dance until the next day. You can always call a cab and ask the driver to take you to one of the clubs indicated above if you have the urge to dance.

Dry Martini Phone number: 932 17 50 72 Address: Carrer d'Aribau, 162-166, Barcelona, Spain, 08036 Hours: Monday through Thursday, 1PM-2:30AM, Friday, 1PM-3AM, Saturday, 6:30PM-3AM, and Sunday, 6:30PM-2:30AM

Join a Pub Crawl or an Amazing Bar.

Joining a bar or a pub crawl is an excellent opportunity to explore the fantastic Catalan nightlife, especially if you are traveling alone. A tour guide and a group of tourists from different countries are participating in this event to get to know Barcelona's party scene. Everyone gets together and visits several bars while enjoying traditional drinks and learning more about both the city and them.

The fact that the directory is up-to-date on the greatest bars and pubs' locations as well as their drink specialties is crucial. You simply need to put your caution aside and go exploring with other tourists who share your enthusiasm for exploring Barcelona's nightlife.

You only need to go through the options in Barcelona's Pub Crawls to select the one that best suits your needs and interests. A great option is the Original Pub Crawl Barcelona and if you want to learn more about it, have a look at the reviews available on getyourguide.com.

These are just a few of the entertaining things you can do at night in the lovely city of Barcelona. Nevertheless, based on how long your trip is, you can expand your list of fantastic ways to experience Barcelona's vibrant nightlife by include additional fascinating events and parties.

Souvenirs and Gifts

Barcelona has a wide selection of unusual gifts and souvenirs that encapsulate the character and essence of the city. These goods, which range from traditional handicrafts to regional gourmet foods, make wonderful keepsakes of your vacation or considerate presents for friends and family back home. Popular mementos and presents include:

5. **Modernist-inspired ceramics**: A variety of ceramic objects, including ornamental tiles, plates, and trinkets, that make for lovely and distinctive mementos have been influenced by Barcelona's modernist architecture, particularly the works of Antoni Gaud.
6. **Catalan wines and cava**: A bottle of local wine or cava, which Catalonia is well renowned for producing, provides a lovely present that the recipient can enjoy long after the vacation has ended. To find a variety of regional wines, visit wine shops or neighborhood markets.
7. **Gourmet food items**: Barcelona has a recognized culinary culture, and there are many gourmet foods available there that are ideal presents, such

premium olive oil, handmade chocolates, or traditional turron (a type of nougat).
8. **Handmade leather goods**: Given the city's reputation for workmanship, you may get handmade leather goods like wallets, belts, and bags in a variety of artisan stores and markets located all over the place.

Barcelona Maps

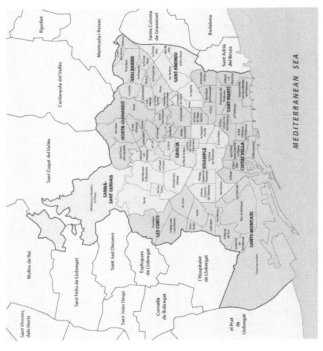

Conclusion

Barcelona is unquestionably one of the most fascinating and vibrant cities in Spain, if not all of Europe! On the list of the top travel destinations in Spain, it competes with Milan and Madrid.

As we reach the end of our tour of Barcelona's charming districts, delectable cuisine, and dynamic culture, it is abundantly evident that this city has something to offer everyone. Barcelona is a treasure mine of experiences waiting to be found, with everything from its renowned architectural masterpieces and sun-kissed beaches to its bustling markets and world-class museums.

Barcelona never fails to enthrall, whether you're a first-time visitor or a seasoned traveler returning for another taste of Catalonia's city. The city provides a wealth of chances for exploration, relaxation, and adventure thanks to its rich history, mild Mediterranean environment, and friendly residents.

Let this travel guide serve as your compass as you set out on your Barcelona trip. It will point you in the direction of remarkable experiences and memories that you won't forget long after you've returned home. Don't be surprised if you find yourself yearning to return to

Barcelona's enchanting streets time and time again as you immerse yourself in the city's energetic atmosphere and variety of attractions.

References:

images: Freepik.com.

The images within this book were chosen using resources from Freepik.com

Manufactured by Amazon.ca
Acheson, AB